Szulem "Sol" Silberzweig

Mama, It Will Be Alright!

A Story of Survival

Edited by
Lilian Gillard and Ingrid Rockberger
of Docostory Ltd., Raanana, Israel.

© 2005 Yad Vashem
P.O.B. 3477, Jerusalem 91034
Email: publications.marketing@yadvashem.org.il

ISBN 965-308-245-0

Typesetting: Gary Rimmer
Production: Docostory Ltd., Raanana, Israel
Printed in Israel, 2005
By Ravgon, Herzlia Pituach.

Dedication

In memory of Szulem "Sol" Silberzweig (1917-2004)
and Gitel "Gloria" Rosen Silberzweig (1922-1979),
their families and the millions of people killed by
the barbaric actions of the Germans and their
collaborators.

We should never let this happen again.

For the last few years of his life, Sol (Szulem) Silberzweig was working on his autobiography – determined to leave a record of his life for his family and the Jewish people.

Sol epitomizes the Jewish fighter and survivor as we read of his heroic actions in the Warsaw ghetto as he saves members of his family, in the seven concentration camps he survived, and later, in the United States, when he stood up to the Union.

His story is tragically typical of many Jews living in Europe during the Second World War. The youngest of seven children, he was born in Warsaw in 1922 to a traditional Jewish family, who had been in the fur business for four generations.

When the war broke out in 1939, 22-year old Sol was already 'in the business'. Trapped in the Warsaw ghetto, he met a childhood sweetheart, Gloria (Gittel). Their lives were intertwined throughout the war as both went from concentration camp to concentration camp, suffering incredible hardships. At war's end, traveling all around Europe, Sol found his Gittel, and the couple married.

Arriving in the US in 1949, Sol set up a fur business and fighting the American Unions along the way, established a successful, international company. Tragically and ironically, while on a business trip in Germany, Gittel was killed in a car accident.

Although badly injured and devastated at the loss of his beloved wife, Sol gradually recovers both mentally and physically and continues to work well into his old age.

CONTENTS

Chapter 1
Childhood Memories

I was born in Warsaw, the youngest of seven children. My oldest sister Henne was born in 1900. My brother, Yakob, was born in 1901, followed by my sister Zosia, (Zelda) in 1906, my brother Monyek in 1908, Leibel (Leon) in 1910, and Salla was born in 1912. Unexpected, I arrived into the world on March 15, 1917. I was named Szulem, which means 'peace'.

At home, I was called Shulem Silberzweig. Home at that time was at 7 Stafke Street, where we lived until 1929, when we moved to a seven-roomed apartment at Pcheyast 9, where we also had a fur factory, "Silberzweig and Sons." It was a better neighborhood and a bigger apartment; we needed a bigger apartment since my brother Monyek came back from the army. Our family had been in the fur business for four generations. My father was born into the fur business that his father and grandfather had established. He traveled to Russia to buy Russian furs to bring to Zamucz, the city where he was born. It was famous for being the hometown of the writer, I.L. Peretz.

As a young man, my father decided it was time to leave Zamucz, and went to visit family in Warsaw to check out the business opportunities. Later, he became very successful in the fur business in Warsaw.

When I was a youngster, I remember that whenever a Jewish holiday came - be it Rosh Hashana, Passover, or a Friday night or Saturday, there were always many family members and friends at our home. My brothers, except my oldest brother Yacob who was in Germany, my sisters, my nieces, and my mother's family would all sit round the table to eat. My father was not an Orthodox Jew, but he had a deep Jewish faith. Near Stafke Street there was a big *shul* (synagogue) located at Pocorna 4. My father often brought *orchim* (guests) to our house, so they could share in the meal; he told us that it was a big *mitzvah* (good deed) from G-d to invite guests.

I went to a school on Kupyetska 39 called Stchurik, a private Jewish Gymnasium well known in the Jewish community. Around 1934 or 1935 we moved to a very nice place called the Landes Building at Franciscana 12. My brother Monyek got married and started his own fur business.

My family employed traveling salesmen who went around Poland with the furs that we made. We imported skins from America that were sought-after in Poland and also exported good furs from Poland: Stonemartin, Ponies and others. At that time there were very small ponies with a lot of markings on their skin; it was very popular in the USA. We also imported skunks, opossum and muskrat. Not many people were importing and exporting furs like we were, you could count on one hand the number of people who were doing business like us. It was not long before everyone knew about us. Later, we opened a store on Myadova Street, a very prominent street in Warsaw, known for its furs. We were very successful. As for Monyek, he started out on his own and also did well for himself.

I was still a youngster, tall and handsome according

to others, and I had started to dress nicely. During these times, people went to dancing school. My friend talked me in to going to such a school on Zamerhof. Every weekend there was a *Deptak* (taking a walk), where young people went to meet each other. The place was called Platsteatralne. I enjoyed dancing; after all I was young.

I haven't mentioned my mother yet. My mother Rachel was born at Geisha 39 in Warsaw. Her mother was Faigele the *Hayben* (midwife), a very good and kind person; she was famous for collecting money and products from wealthy people for her services and giving them to the needy. Unlike many Jewish girls and boys, Bubbe Feigele was able to study at a university in Poland; she worked with the famous Dr. Soloveichik, a surgeon who was very well known all over Europe. It was a big *yiches* (honor) to be a friend of Dr. Soloveichik. She was very unique.

When my father met my mother, she was as beautiful as an aristocrat. She had two sisters, Leah and Tobe. Leah married a fine man and they moved to Argentina. Tobe worked in Warsaw and was separated from her husband. She had a daughter, Pesha, who spent most of her time in our house. Before Leah went to Argentina, I remember how she and Tobe and the whole family used to sit around the table at our home on the holidays and the Sabbath. Time passed and the borders of Argentina were opened to refugees. Adults could go but without their children. Tobe came to my mother and told her about it. My mother said, "Leave your daughter Pesha with me, maybe you can send for her in a little while." So Pesha came to live with us like another daughter. Letters went back and forth, and in 1935 she was able to join her mother in Argentina.

My father had two brothers and one sister who lived in Zamucz, where business was not too good. My Uncle Daniel came to my father in Warsaw and told him that in America, life was very good, in the "Goldene Land." By this time my father was very well off, a success in the fur business. We were importing and exporting, relying on common sense to run the business. My father told his brother that if he wanted to go, he would give him the money for the shipcard (ticket). My father said he should go and "*macht vi du vislt.*" Later, Daniel wrote a letter about how he liked it in America and suggested that Surah Leah, and Yisruel go too. My father bought the tickets for them both.

I remember when I was quite young and living in Stafke there were Polish boys who tried to beat up the Jewish boys. They used to say to us, "*Zhide, go to Palestine.*" But we were young and strong, and we ran after them and beat them up. After this, they never bothered us again. In general, at this time in Poland there was a lot of anti-Semitism. At night it was very dangerous to walk around in the streets. If a young gentile man from the University saw a Jewish person walking alone, he would beat him up. When Pilsudski was Marshal in Poland, no one dared do these things because he was a friend of the Jewish people, ever since a Jewish family in Lodz hid him when the Russians were after him. When Marshal Smigly-Ridz took over, things changed; he was very anti-Semitic. He was bad for the Jews and his negative influence extended up until the wartime.

There were several businesses like ours. Most handled either skins or garments but we did both. I was thirteen when I started to learn about the business. I ran around the factory and learned what everyone was doing. I liked the fur business because in Europe it was very prestigious. We walked around with white aprons just like a dentist or a doctor. The fur business was special, not like just being a tailor or a shoemaker.

Once my father's cousin called him. He had a fabric store in Zamucz – silk, wool and other materials; he asked my father if his son, Falek Silberzweig, could come to him to learn the fur business. My father said OK, and so Falek was sent to us. Falek was a few years older than me, and I had never seen him before. Gradually he started to learn the fur business. At that time my brother Monyek was the main cutter in the factory.

After a while, Falek wanted to strike out on his own. He went to some furriers in Bigdosh on the border with Germany where he worked for someone else. It was hard for me when he left because we had become friends. My father said, "See! He learned from me and now he's going off to work for another retailer."

Sol's father and brother

The family

Pesha Silberzweig

Aunt Sarah Frida,
New York,
before the war

Brother Jack, 1920

Sol (r) and Alois Pozikski

Gloria at age 14

Chapter 2
The Bombardment of Warsaw

September 1, 1939, I was 22 years old. It was the summer time, and we were all enjoying ourselves in our country summerhouse in Mechalin, 40 kilometers from Warsaw. On weekends, the whole family was there: my father and mother, my sister Henne and her husband Max and their two children Dadek and Kuba, my sister Zelda with her husband Semek Cooperberg and their young son Felix, my brother Monyek and his wife Edja, and their daughter, whose name I can't remember. Then came my sister Salla with her husband, Monyek Gus, and their daughter. And of course, I was there too.

At Mechalin we heard news. We didn't hear it from the radio. Nobody had radios. And we didn't hear it from the television. There was no television yet; the news was announced over a loud speaker: A war had started and Germany had invaded Poland. People wanted to run away from the big cities but we wanted to get home to Warsaw. We didn't realize that being out of the city was better. We thought being in the city would be better, but it ended up being a terrible mistake. We managed to engage a horse and buggy from farmers and, putting all the summer stuff on it, headed back to Warsaw.

At the time the war broke out my eldest brother, Yakob Silberzweig, was already in America. He ran away with a friend to Germany in 1919, to avoid serving in the Polish army.

When we got back home to Warsaw everything was on fire from the bombing, people were running around like crazy trying to buy food, but it was almost impossible; even things like sugar. Candles were being bought up as if it was for a blackout. People were talking about what might happen. It didn't take long until we found out. After only three or four days, bombs started falling all over Warsaw. The entire Jewish quarter was burned in this attack. The Germans knew where to bomb. They knew that the Jews were concentrated in one area of the city, the Jewish Quarter, and they lived and had their businesses there.

The building we lived in at 12 Franciscana Street was also occupied by gentiles; it was very beautiful and we were happy there. Our family was well off and we had a good life. All of my siblings were married; I was the only one still at home. The business was at 25 Myadova Street, the store upstairs. The factory was just up the road at 27.

I can see it all so clearly, as if it were yesterday: The Jewish Quarter and bombs falling, the whole sky lit up as the place burned. Many people were killed and many lay dying in the streets, calling and screaming out for their loved ones, anyone, to help them.

For two whole weeks the bombing continued with no let up. Poland did not respond. Day and night the bombs fell. A bomb fell in the courtyard of the apartment building where we lived. Luckily no one was hurt. My father was a very thoughtful and kind man. Every night he went out to help the sick. I will always remember one day in particular, he had just left our building and had almost reached the big square when the bombs fell. Shrapnel flew everywhere, catching people as they ran for shelter. The scene was bloody, people lying down and screaming in agony. My father took sheets from the house, ripped them up and made bandages to help the injured. I ran outside and saw this horrible sight, but I was not scared. I was angry, angry at Hitler, and at what the Germans were doing. In the area where the Jews lived were several German factories. I found out later that some people in the factories had signaled to the planes informing them where the Jews lived.

Ten days before the Germans marched into Warsaw, the Polish factory owners ran away. They were liquidating everything the Jews had. Later when the Poles surrendered the bombing stopped. Many people ran away. The Polish army discarded their uniforms and tried to hide them from the Germans, passing themselves off as civilians. Those that were found were shipped off to the camps.

By now people were going hungry, starving. We tried to organize something to eat. It was very hard. Bakery shops had not baked for weeks. Nobody knew what to do. One day, when a bakery shop around the corner began baking, long lines began to form outside; people stood waiting to buy a loaf of bread. Even as early as 5 AM, I saw black bread in the window ready to be sold. I kicked in the cellar window of the bakery and took two loaves home to my parents. I will never forget that day; they were so happy with the bread.

After a few days we had nothing to eat again. We had just returned from the country and, not knowing what to expect in the city, we did not bring back any supplies. In the past Polish farmers used to come into the Jewish quarter, their farms were nearby and so they would bring eggs, chickens and ducks.

The following day I managed to *shlep* (carry) on my back a whole sack of rice from one of the warehouses that belonged to the Poles. I caught a soldier trying to steal two sacks of rice. When I told him that I would report him he gave me one sack and kept one for himself. I gave a farmer a small bag of rice for which he gave me two ducks. My mother made a big *metziah* (bargain) with these ducks. She took off the fat and broiled it… what a delicacy! We couldn't tell anyone this story.

My siblings lived close by and we tried to see each other everyday. We often talked about trying to leave Poland but we did not want to leave the business and our stock behind. And anyway, no one wanted to make the effort to leave. No one knew what was to come.

I was young, but I remember how in 1939, people were being caught by the Germans in Warsaw and sent away, or were shot on the streets. Seeing this I decided like many others to try and run away. One of my sister's sister-in-law Ruzia had family in Bialystok. "Come with me and we will go over to the Russians," she said to me. This was probably at the end of September. Poland was divided in two – one half was under German rule, and through an agreement with Stalin, the other half became Russian. Bialystok was in the Russian half on the other side of the Buk River. At the age of 22 you are an adult, so of course my parents let me go. My father allowed me to take some of the furs with me to sell, so I put some furs into a sack and some I concealed on myself by wearing shirts on top of them.

Along with about six or seven other people we were

smuggled to the border. Ruzia left her husband with the children and went by herself to her family in Bialystok; people were already saying that things were better on the Russian side. Ruzia, who looked just like a *shikseh* (gentile woman), dressed me so I would look like a gentile too.

In Warsaw, there was no ghetto at that time; it was still the beginning. The trains were running as normal. I traveled with Ruzia and another couple on the train. The train stopped at a small town before Sarnok. The day before, the Germans had come to this very town and killed a Jewish man and his nine sons. They were hanged in the town square. They were the smugglers who took people over the river to the Russian side. It was the Poles spying for the Germans who told them how these Jews were smuggling other Jews over to the Russians. I was being smuggled by the Poles. It was from them I heard how they were jealous of the Jews claiming they were taking away their work. That was the reason for their telling the Germans. They told this to us even though they knew we were Jewish, since only Jews were being smuggled across.

Soon, the train approached another town called Shedletz, on the German side of the border. I looked through the window; it was nighttime and by the light of the moon I could just make out the river in the distance. When we left the train we had to walk along a back road; a horse and buggy was supposed to meet us along the way. "There it is!" I heard someone whisper.

A short drive in the buggy and we arrived at the riverside. We waited in the darkness. The Poles were coming with a boat and we were to travel overnight to the other side of the River Buk. It was very dangerous; the Germans were using dogs to try to catch people. Anyone could have been caught.

The boat, called a *plimp*, which looked more like a raft, seemed to take forever until it reached the other side. It was quite a distance, further than from New York to New Jersey. When we finally disembarked, one of our party thought they heard dogs barking. We held our breath, afraid to make even the slightest sound.

"OK," someone else said. "It was just the wind blowing. Let's go."

We walked through the woods. It was very muddy but we didn't care. We were just pleased that we were getting away from the Germans. We walked the whole night, people resting a little and then walking on some more. We walked sixty kilometers overnight, trying hard to stick together.

The sun was coming up when we arrived at a town. We found a restaurant in the town run by Jews, and they gave us food. The Jews arrived in this town after the start of the war. "*Shlomi, Yanke, vus machste,*" (how are you?) you could hear people shouting at each other. From this town we took a train to Bialystok. There was no longer a need to be afraid of the Germans. Bialystok was being run by the Russians. They didn't have a lot of food, but more than in Warsaw. It was like night and day, you did not have to worry that someone might shoot you; everyone was free to do or say whatever they wanted. Bialystok, at this time, had not been bombed, it was later that the Germans bombed the town when they fought the Russians. At this point in time, it was protected by the pact between Hitler and Stalin.

One day, I happened to see the very famous cantor and opera singer, Moishe Kosovitsky. He was there with his family. Quite by chance, while I was in Bialystok, I saw my cousin Felix on my father's side. He had been a big shot in Warsaw - he owned a company that manufactured ladies' clothes. He too ran away and left his wife and daughter behind in Warsaw. At that time, many people thought that the Germans were only looking for the men, and so it was safe to leave the women and children behind. How naïve we were.

I was in Bialystok about three or four weeks and thought that life there was very good. We decided to go home and tell my parents to pack up all their belongings and come and live there. I didn't say anything to Felix, but I told Ruzia, and together we planned to return to Warsaw.

Getting back to the German side was not so easy. We walked, hitched a ride with someone who had a horse and buggy and then walked some more. We went through Malkin, a town near Treblinka. (It was only later that I found out that Treblinka was nearby.) It began to snow. Light snow at first, and then the wind started whipping it up until it felt like a blizzard, blowing in our eyes making it difficult to see where we were going. Ruzia wanted to stop and take shelter under some bushes. "We're almost at the border," I told her. "We'll stop when we get to the other side."

All of a sudden there was the sound of dogs barking. Felix had told me that SS German officers with giant dogs patrolled the borders. Then we caught sight of them. SS officers were running with wolf dogs on the leash trying to catch someone. Ruzia and I waited until the dogs were chasing someone else and then we managed to get across the border without being detected. By this time the river was frozen and we had to travel by land. Some people did try to walk over the river and fell in. We decided to go all the way around instead.

We made it back to Warsaw at the end of November. When I got back to my parents I was greeted with "shulem aleichems". I told them how everyone was living like human beings in Bialystok. Not like in Warsaw, where they were catching people and taking them behind the parliament, "sym" house, and just shooting them because they didn't like the way they looked. I suggested to my family that they come back with me to Bialystok, but my father said, "No. Let's wait and see." He didn't know what to do with all the merchandise, or how to hide it and what would be a safe way to leave. My father's decision to stay proved fatal.

Not long after, the Germans were catching people on the street and sending them away; nobody had any idea to where.

Chapter 3
Meeting Gittel, and Life in the Warsaw Ghetto

I was still living with my parents at Franciscana 12, but we couldn't continue with the business. The Germans announced over the loud speaker that everybody had to bring any furs they had to the police station. We hid the furs in double walls that we created. Life was very difficult. People became very afraid. One day the superintendent of the building informed us that an order had been issued to all the residents of the building: All the Jews must leave but all the gentiles could stay. We were moved into the ghetto, which started at Franciscana 10. We found an apartment at Franciscana 24.

Some men were sent away. My father being an older man thought that they would not touch him, but he was very worried about my brother Monyek and he went to warn him not to go out and risk getting caught. Hours went by. My mother waited anxiously by the window hoping to catch a glimpse of him walking along the street towards the house. We all waited. He never came back. Monyek told us later that our father never arrived. He must have been caught and taken somewhere on the way. We did not know anything yet about the concentration camps, so that thought didn't enter our minds. We thought that he had been shot and killed, or taken for slave labor.

It was 1941 and we were living in the ghetto. Walls were going up all around, as more and more Jews began moving into the ghetto. The Germans would come to the ghetto to take people away. We had to constantly be on the alert not to be caught on the street. Some Jews were even assigned the job of helping build the walls, even those who had never built anything before.

The ghetto was rapidly closing us in, every day another wall went up. I had managed to find work in the Schultz factory, which was producing vests for the German pilots. I was able to get this work because my brother Leibel's neighbor was the General Manager of Schultz. His name was Topelson. Another reason was I could bring my own sewing machine, which I had used for the furs. Everyday I traveled by tram with Monyek to and from the factory.

It was about a week before the ghetto was closed, that I met up with an old friend of mine, Gittel. I had first met Gittel in 1935 in Mechalin, a place with villas where people spent several months in the summer until they came back to the city. I was staying there with my parents and Henne in *Rubenstein's Villas* (which belonged to the family of the pianist Arthur Rubenstein. One of the family members used to play the piano on the porch early in the morning.) Gittel and her parents were also spending the summer there.

I had gone to the place where they had play machines. There she was, this beautiful young girl of about 12 years old. With her blonde hair, green eyes and rosy red cheeks she looked like a *shikseh*. She was not called Gloria in those days; to everyone she was Gittel Rosen. I asked her if she wanted to play on the machines with me. She said that she did not have any more money, so I suggested we go for an ice cream. She was with a friend. I could see that I was not going to be alone with her, so I took both of them out. Over a bowl of vanilla ice cream I found out, to my delight, that Gittel was also staying in one of *Rubenstein's Villas*.

She told me her family was in the shoe business and I told her my family was in the fur business. "Oh", she said, "the fur business." In Poland in those days being in the fur business was a *yiches* (a big deal). During our stay in Mechalin we talked a lot, and sometimes we just played around. Gittel had beautiful long blonde hair and sometimes I would tease her by throwing pine needles (*koltani*) at her, which would stick in her hair. She hated that and for a while would not talk to me. The more time we spent together the more I wanted to kiss her. Eventually, I tried, but she was not very pleased about it.

We saw each other on and off until the war broke out. I liked Gittel very much and we were good friends. I always felt so proud when she walked with me on the streets of Warsaw, people would turn their heads and make comments. She always wore beautiful dresses made to order by the dressmaker and not store bought. Once she wanted to have a blue costume with black broadtail fur trim made, and she came to me with the designs. "How much will it cost?" she asked. I looked at her and said, "We'll see!"

My mother said, "Who is this girl to you, and why didn't you give her a price?" I told her that she would pay me later and that she was my girlfriend.

We went out a lot after that, people were always pointing at her and commenting how beautiful she was and how she looked like an angel. I once asked her why

27

she always dressed so fancy. "Because I like to be well dressed!" she said.

Her father, Moishele Rosen, was a very fine man and often invited me to Friday night dinners with them. He had five *Sefer Torahs*, (scrolls of the Law) which he purchased to keep in the *shul*. He would take people off the street to *daven mincha* (pray/attend the afternoon service) and *maariv* (the evening service) and give them a drink and a snack just for coming in and *davening* (praying). When I went to their house I always brought a gift of halva, dried fruit, or pastries.

About a week before the bombing of Warsaw, Gittel's whole family came from Praga to stay with my family for a short time. It was around the time when Jews were being expelled from Praga. Now Gittel and her family came back to live in the ghetto. I was very happy to see her again, and so was my mother. She was glad to have friends nearby.

The ghetto was still not closed in; they built the gates later, after all the Jews had moved in. Soon the unthinkable happened: Jews were separated. We were sealed in. By the end of November 1941, the ghetto was closed. It had become a sealed ghetto. Everybody who was working at the Schultz factory continued to work there but without pay. I worked for them every day in order to preserve my life. It was simple. If you didn't work, you were taken away. They took many people out of the ghetto and sent them to Treblinka.

We moved from the ghetto area to the Schultz factory in 1941. I worked there until 1943. When Gloria's father, Moshe Rosen, died, I arranged for her mother and sisters to come to the Schultz area from the ghetto.

I found them a nice apartment, and paid some money to people to help arrange for their move.

German civilians ran the Schultz factory. The factory area had been cleaned out of residents earlier and there were many empty buildings. The people who lived there had been sent to the camps. Schultz owned the factory and was probably linked to the SS, or he would not have been able to own the factory. Vermacht people were inside the factory, under the control of Schultz.

In the factory we were treated like prisoners, movement was limited and we were not paid. We worked hard all day and received only soup! We came in the morning from the area outside and were given a cup of coffee made from *cikoria* (chicory). They let us leave around 6 PM. I was a fur cutter; if you left your position, people would start to look for you and inquire as to your whereabouts. You were allowed to call in sick just like at a regular job, however, if you didn't work, you would be sent away and you would never be heard from again! Work was essential for survival.

By this time, Gittel and I were in love, she was sixteen years old and I was twenty. Our romance was overshadowed by the news that there was going to be an *aktsia* (in WWII - round-up of Jews prior to deportation to concentration camps) to take away many of the people who were not working in the factory.

My mother, my sister-in-law and her child were not working at the factory, and so a solution had to be found how to keep them safe. They had to hide somewhere, but where? We had to act quickly, since we knew that the SS would not take long until they came searching for the people who were not working.

There were two or three rooms where we were living with very large European style closets. My mother went to the back of the closet and together we removed the back-board. Before our eyes lay the solution. Behind the closet was a room. "Come on, everyone," said my mother, "quickly!" We entered the closet and came through into the other room. I took a feather bed cover and ripped it up to make it look like the place was abandoned. I felt sure the SS would be reluctant to search any further when they saw this. We also hid Gittel's mother's sister and brother in the same manner, but in a different building. The closets were moved in front of the door of the next room, so people could pass through but it would give the appearance of being up against a plain wall. Then we ripped blankets again and spread some garbage around for authenticity.

I managed to get down to our courtyard just before the SS officers came. They were either Ukrainian or Lithuanians, the worst murderers. They called for everyone to come down. In the courtyard there was a blacksmith, he gave me a black shirt and I made my face dirty to look as if I had been working. I stood with a hammer hitting the hot iron. Anyone not working would have been taken away by the SS. From inside the building came the sound of a child crying. The officers heard him and they ran to see who it was. What happened next made my blood freeze. Laughing, they took the child by the feet and burned him with their cigarette lighters. The child screamed with pain, and they thought that it was funny. I saw this and I wanted to help the child but did not dare to. I felt less than human that day. I wanted to do something but I pretended to work so they did not take me away. But I saw it. The picture of that horrible scene has stayed with me.

The officers had gathered up some people; one tried to run away but one of the officers chased after him and caught him. He was pushed roughly into a line with the others and then taken away. They were marched outside the gate, which was being guarded by armed gendarmes and two Jewish police officers. This was to make sure that no one came in or went out of the Schultz compound. The Jewish police were trying to get in with the Polish police and the SS.

Several months passed and there was another *aktsia*. We were horrified when they began clearing out all the extra people: everybody who was not working, elderly women and children. Gittel's mother, her two sisters and baby brother were all taken away and we never saw them again. At that time, by sheer luck Gittel was visiting my mother and sister-in-law. My mother begged her to stay with us. "You'll get caught and taken away!" my mother warned her.

A few weeks later, the SS came again and cleared everyone out of the Schultz compound, this time including the workers. We were taken to a big circle. They blocked a whole area called "the cauldron" (*Kociol* in Polish).[1] Then the SS handed out tickets. The men who worked at Schultz were given either a yellow or a green ticket to put on their lapel. I got a green ticket and my brother Monyek got a yellow one. I worried

[1] *A word literally translated as "cauldron". This was how the residents of the ghetto referred to the streets to which they were confined during the selections, as well as to the narrow area in which the Jews receiving work cards were permitted to live following the "Great Aktion."*

about what was going to happen to me, and my family. I felt sick with worry. I found out soon enough.

We found out what the different colored tickets represented from people who were hanging around by the gates. A green ticket sent you back to Schultz. A yellow ticket meant you would go to the *Umschlagplatz* (transfer point), and board a train bound for Treblinka. The reason I received a green ticket and Monyek a yellow one was that I was young and strong. My brother was older and lost his hearing in one ear in a bombing. A sickening feeling swept over me. My mother, sister-in-law, and the baby, and others, all had yellow tickets. They were all going to die!

Everyone was crying, terrified to think what his or her fate was going to be. This was the time when people started to be taken away, and we first learned about Treblinka. At first nobody wanted to believe that it was true that Jews were being gassed. After all, we thought, the Germans were educated people, weren't they? How could they do such a thing?

From out of nowhere, an idea came to me. I gave the green ticket to Monyek and told him to use it to go back to the Schultz factory. There was a Jewish police captain there that I knew, by the name of Henyek. I knew that if anyone could help us Henyek could. My idea was that Monyek would give my green ticket to Henyek and ask him to bring it back to me. This way we would both be able to go back to Schultz with only one green ticket.

I told Monyek that we would wait in a house at Mila 47. I had a feeling that my idea would work

Monyek met up with Henyek and told him his name

and that he was my brother, and that I had a yellow ticket. "Salek needs a green ticket or he'll be sent away to the *Umschlagplatz*. Please help him, Henyek," Monyek pleaded with him.

I was waiting in the house at Mila 47. Suddenly, I saw Henyek. He greeted me with a big smile, hugged and kissed me. He gave me back the green ticket and left. My plan had worked!

Now I still had to do something to save my mother, Gittel, and Monyek's wife, Edja, and their baby. I found out that in that building there was a bakery. Downstairs there was a cellar full of sacks of flour. That's it, I thought, this is a good place to hide! I took them down there, as well as Mrs. Kaplan, our neighbor from Schultz, and her baby.

The place was very dirty, and alive with rats. In the center of the cellar was an enormous stone. With a lot of pushing and shoving we managed to close off the room where they were hiding with a stone. Now I had to get out of the "cauldron" and get through the checkpoints of the gendarmes, the Polish police and the Jewish police guarding the gates. I didn't want to go alone because they would suspect me. So I waited until a group of people passed and went with them.

I came back alone to Monyek's house in order to get some sleep. I was tired and hungry. I knew I would have to bring my family back to Schultz as soon as possible before they were taken to the *Umschlagplatz* and Treblinka. I lay down on the bed, and all of a sudden I had an idea. On Nowolipie Street on the same street as Schultz there was a big bakery, where the bread was baked for the Schultz factory. The bread was taken from the bakery with a horse and cart, called a *forgan* in Polish, the cart having a sliding door. When you opened the sliding door there was a divider where the bread was piled up. My idea was to take the horse and cart down to Mila 47 as if to bring flour from the bakery in that building, hide my family inside the wagon, covering them up with sacks of flour, and smuggle them to Schultz. If anyone opened the door, all they would see would be the sacks. I knew the Vermacht soldier working for Schultz who was watching the comings and goings from the factory.

I told Monyek my plan and he said it was impossible. "*Bist a meshigene*" (you are crazy), he said. I decided to go ahead with it regardless. I hoped it could work and anyway we had to try something.

Five hundred *zloty* and a gold piece secured the permit to bring the flour from the bakery at Mila 47 to Schultz. I asked the soldier to come with me to the bakery, collect the flour and go back with it to Schultz. We went to the bakery and said that we had come to collect flour for the Schultz factory. The soldier took the horse and wagon, and he gave me a Vermacht jacket and a white apron with a permit to get flour. I was holding the reins and the soldier was next to me. SS were standing all around the *Kociol* – no one could go in or out. The soldier showed the permit to take flour to Schultz, and we were in. The building at 47 Mila had a courtyard and all the people were looking at the soldier and at me wearing the Vermacht jacket like we came from outer space. They couldn't believe their eyes.

I went down to the cellar and we pushed the stone out of the way. I explained the plan to my family.

"Don't take too much," I told them, "there's only a limited amount of space." I began helping them into the wagon, along with two very large sacks of flour. If the gendarmes decided to open the wagon door all they would see would be the sacks of flour and they would think that everything was kosher.

My mother, who was 62 at the time, said it would be a miracle if we succeeded. I said "Mama, listen to me, listen to Shulemel, with God's help, it will be alright." People started coming over, offering us money to take them in the wagon as well. A man came with a little sack with ten gold $20 coins and asked me to take his daughter to Schultz. He pushed the pouch of gold into my hands, begging me to take her. What could I do? I told him to keep his money and that I'd take the girl.

We started on our way, but reached only as far as the Lubetskiego gate, when we heard a voice from behind shout out. "HALT! HALT! Where are you going?" It was a gendarme.

I felt sick to my stomach. I prayed that nobody hidden inside the wagon would make a sound. I stopped the wagon and waited, my heart pounding. I glanced behind. Two gendarmes approached, their guns pointing towards the back of the wagon. Apparently there was a Jew trying to sneak out by hanging on to the back of our wagon. They dragged him off and took him to Geisha Street 39. Coincidentally, this was where my grandmother, Bubbe Feige used to live. It was as if she was looking out for us. Suddenly the air was filled with the sound of shots being fired and we were sure they'd shot that Jew.

When I heard this, I didn't wait, I made the horses

gallop all the way back to Schultz, which was five blocks away. Some people were waiting around in the courtyard at Nowolipie 30. When I opened the wagon in the courtyard and took out the flour everybody thought there was only flour in the wagon. When they saw people coming out of the wagon, everyone started cheering. "Look what Shulemel did. He's a genius." I told everyone that the idea came to me like a message from heaven. It came to me in a dream. I was very proud of myself. Later on I thought what if I had been caught? They would have shot me and everybody else. It was just luck that we all made it through. Maybe they took the man that was hanging on the back of the wagon instead of us as a sacrifice to save my mother, my sister-in-law, Gittel, and the kids. I told my mother that I was sure that Bubbe Feige helped to save us.

We gave the flour to the bakers, who were delighted to receive such a large amount of flour.

At this point, Gittel found out that her mother Rifka, two sisters (Ruzia and Henne) and brother (Monyck) were no longer at Schultz. She was very distraught. To try to calm her down my mother attempted to convince her that they had been taken somewhere else to work. My brother felt that my return with the family was nothing short of a miracle. He told me I was *meshigeh* (crazy) to try to do it and could not believe that it had actually worked.

Chapter 4
My Family's Fate

My brother Leibel lived on Leshna Street with his wife Yadja and their three children. He worked for a company called Tebens that made uniforms and collars for the Germans. When the next *aktsia* occurred, people were being taken away from Tebens. They took everyone out of their living quarters and sent them away. When Leibel returned from work to find the place empty, curtains flowing in the wind, clothes ripped all over the floor, he knew right away that his family had been taken away. He was a broken man. Everything he loved in his life was gone. He walked into the children's bedroom and took the baby girl's shoes and shirt and put it against himself and cried. Then he turned himself over to the Nazis to be taken away to the *Umschlagplatz*. They had taken away his wife and children and he didn't want to live anymore. Life was finished for him. We found all this out from someone who knew Leibel. This happened after I brought my family into Schultz with the flour wagon.

* * * * * *

My sister Salla lived with her husband Monyek Guss and their baby girl in the ghetto. Even though we were in Schultz, they preferred to remain where they were. Salla's husband Monyek was working for the Germans in Platsufka, outside the ghetto working on the trains, with iron or loading steel. He was a strong guy. It had been more than a year since we had seen each another. I later learned from other people about what had happened to them.

Around the end of 1941 and the beginning of 1942 the people in the ghetto were told that a new factory was being built called Travnik in the Malkin area near Treblinka, and workers were needed. They were told that they would be out in the fresh air and life would be better. People believed it. They were taking on tailors and other handy workers. Monyek heard about this project and said that maybe they should try to get these jobs.

Afterwards, we found out that Travnik was just a trick to get the Jews out there. As soon as they arrived in the area they were machine-gunned down. Deep ditches were already prepared for the bodies. It did not matter who they were: women, children, they just did not care. It was a trick perpetrated by the Nazis. My sister Salla and her family were murdered this way.

When the news reached me, I couldn't believe it. How could they do this to a fellow human being? Perhaps they just weren't human beings! How could that be? Murdering the innocent in such a brutal cold-blooded way. We were functioning like machines. You cannot put these feelings into words. It was like being an animal.

My sister Zelda and her husband Semek Cooperberg were working in a small factory in the ghetto, manufacturing parts for airplanes. The factory used to be an ORT school for youngsters to learn a trade before the war. One day I found out that they liquidated the factory and sent everyone to Treblinka to be killed, including Zelda, her husband, and their son, Felix. This was also while I was still in Schultz.

My sister Henne was living in the ghetto with her husband Max and her sons Dadek and Kuba. One morning, without prior warning, SS soldiers marched into their building. The soldiers dragged everyone outside: men, women, and children. They were forced to stand for hours in the middle of the street - children crying, their mothers trying to coax them to stop. They had heard how other SS found great pleasure in torturing crying children. Then suddenly they were made to march at gunpoint to the *Umschlagplatz*. From there they were taken to Treblinka and murdered. Kuba jumped off the train on the way to Treblinka. (More about Kuba's fate – later).

Chapter 5
The Ghetto Uprising

We were now back in Schultz in the apartment and had returned to work. Along with some friends of mine, we decided to build an underground bunker, big enough to hold up to eighteen people, at Nowilipie 39, in the back of a bakery. Behind the bakery there was a garden with vegetables and flowers. We built the bunker underneath the garden.

One of us, a plumber, managed to hook up water. His brother was a carpenter and they worked together.

We built the bunker very quietly so no one would know what we were up to. We even set up some pipes to help filter in fresh air. Working day and night in two shifts, the bunker took three months to complete. During this time, there were no other *aktsias* at Schultz.

One day, while visiting Monyek at Nowolipie 23 (I lived at Nowolipie 41), I was handed a piece of paper. It was a message from the underground. I was shocked; until then the underground had never contacted me. They probably heard of what I did to save my family. The note said I should be downstairs at 11 PM. A truck would be coming to take me to a brush factory, which made brushes for the Germans on Shventeyurska Street. I told my family about the note from the underground.

At 11 PM I went downstairs. I looked all around. A guy was waiting for me and he took me to a small truck waiting around the corner with five or six people in it.

On the truck there were barrels covered by a plastic

tarp, to show the guards. We began to drive through the gates. I was frightened that we would be stopped. Someone sitting next to me in the truck, smiled. "Don't worry, we made arrangements with the guards to allow us to leave. There was always one Jewish guard and one gendarme. I looked around inside the truck; they were all nice young boys. As we drove closer to the edge of the ghetto, they told me they had chosen me to help fight in the underground. It was at this point that they gave me a gun.

We stayed in apartments formerly used by people who had been working in the brush factory. There was one building where the entrance went from Shventeyurska 32 to Volova 6; somehow the underground figured out that the Germans were planning to clear out the ghetto in the next few days. They seemed to know that the SS would enter the ghetto through Volova, and so we lined the stones on the street with mines and covered them with dirt.

The underground's information was right. The next morning, the SS did march in, and over one hundred SS soldiers were killed by the mines. The resistance was able to kill many Germans during the course of the uprising. While active in the underground I met Mordechai Anielewicz.

Whenever there was a Jewish holiday, the Nazis would take action against the Jews, when they were praying and giving praise to The Almighty. So, we heard that the first day of Passover was the day they decided to make the ghetto *Juden Rein* (free of Jews).

The next morning when the resistance met up, we were each given an assignment to carry out. I was told to listen to what was going on the other side of Shventeyurska Street. The ghetto wall was built on the street dividing the Jews inside the ghetto and the Poles outside. On the Polish side, there was Krashisky Park (Ogrut Krasinsky).

When the Germans started to bomb the ghetto we were given weapons, and assigned positions to maintain. The bombs rained down on us and all around fires flared up, as buildings burned to the ground. I, along with some other people, ran to shelter in the bunker. I didn't want to die. I wanted to see my family again.

Day and night the bombing continued. When there was a slight let up from the bombing, and we felt safe enough to venture from the bunker, we were met with the horror of seeing burnt people lying around the courtyard: their bodies in grotesque contortions, enveloped in a second by the firebombs. I could not believe my eyes.

There was no means of communication and we were like animals prowling around. I was on the second floor of a building at the ghetto's edge where I could see over the wall. I could see and hear Poles on the other side celebrating the demise of the Jews, and how tomorrow they would be able to go and get all the Jews' furniture for free. They were also excited about getting their down blankets, and chickens, all for nothing.

As the ghetto burned, people started to come out of their bunkers because they were choking. The next day, we found out that there was a guy who claimed to be Jewish and had worked with the SS to report where the Jews were hiding. I went with a few other guys through the attic to a cellar. The man was there. It was at

Franciscana 21. We approached him and asked him about his working with the Germans. He of course denied it, but we had a witness. Some of the other fellows who were with me grabbed him by his throat, choking him until he was almost dead and then beat him until he died. Without any feelings of guilt, although I was a bit shaken, we left him there and went back to our positions in the brush factory

By night we stayed in the bunker and by day we came out to our positions. This was the third or fourth day of the bombing. I was sent into a house that had already been bombed out. We were able to walk from house to house through the attics. I sat upstairs on the third floor. The leader told me to go up very high and check on the Germans' movements. I saw Polish women, prostitutes, working with the SS. They went to the bunkers and encouraged Jews to come out. They would say in Polish, "Come out, the coast is clear." It was while I was there that I heard someone coming up the stairs. I took the gun and hid it behind the bricks. If I had been found with it I would have been shot on sight.

I was scared. Suddenly, someone with a German accent shouted for 'the Jude' to come down. There was no use my hiding there, they would only come and drag me out, and shoot me. I gave myself up, thankful that I had hidden the gun, but I managed later to sneak away and return to the bunker. It was Pesach 1943. I was twenty-six years old.

I decided to try to go back to Schultz during the night to check on my family: my mother, Gittel, Monyek and his wife and child, and the others.

Altogether, eighteen people went into the bunker to hide when I joined the underground.

It was a half hour walk to Schultz. The way was very dark. I did not see another soul. I had to crawl most of the way so the Poles wouldn't see me. (The SS were afraid to come to the ghetto at night.) All the while I was wondering what my family was going through. I was feeling very bad. I was sure that I had lost everything and had nothing more to live for. It was clear that Schultz had been liquidated.

When I arrived at the bunker it was already dawn. It was empty. Everything was ripped up. My family was gone. I saw SS walking in the middle of the street around Schultz, looking for people who may have been hiding. I tried to duck into a corner but they spotted me. I didn't know what to do. I had left the gun in the ghetto so I was unarmed. I pressed my body up hard against the wall hardly daring to breathe. Footsteps approached me, and then someone shouted, "Jude get over here, NOW!" I didn't move, maybe they were talking to some other poor soul, I kidded myself. A face suddenly peered into mine and a hand shot out and roughly grabbed me. "Get in line with the other vermin," an SS soldier spat at me.

All of a sudden I had an idea: when I was with the underground on Shventeyurska Street I saw a cellar full of furs. I decided to try my luck: I told the SS that I had a lot of furs hidden somewhere and I could take him to the place. He "bought" it. He took me in a car with a few other SS, and I took them to the furs. They took the furs and let me go. Shventeyurska Street was empty; all the people I knew were gone.

I stood like a statue. I was alone. No mother, no brother, no Gittel. I was alone. I decided to give myself up. There was only one place to go - the *Umschlagplatz*. I didn't know at that time where the people were being sent from the *Umschlagplatz*.

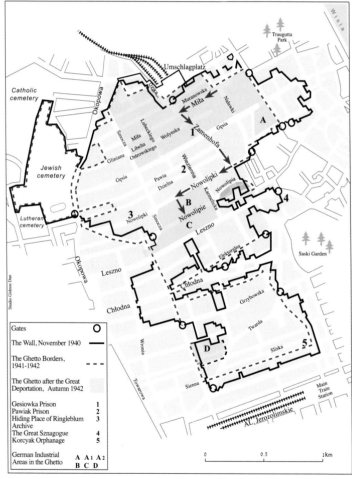

The Flight Route

Chapter 6
Treblinka and Majdanek

We arrived at the *Umschlagplatz*. I saw death before my eyes. People were lying on the asphalt crying "*Shma Israel*, (Hear O' Israel), help us."

We waited by the railway tracks. The Ukrainians in their black uniforms were treating everyone like animals. They were shouting at people – things like "Shut up or I will kill your baby right now." There was a big hole in the asphalt for going to the bathroom. I told myself that it was impossible to run away at this point. I wished that I had died in Schultz, it was surely better than being here and the fate that awaited me.

The next morning a train arrived with SS people on it. Those who remained alive were grabbing at whatever they could. We were made to line up alongside the tracks. The train arrived and we were loaded into the cattle cars, about 2000 people in all, approximately 120 people standing in each car of the train. There was no room for anybody to even sit down. On the floor of the cars, chlorine, and a white powder for disinfection, had been scattered. The smell was making everyone sick. The doors were slammed shut and we were on our way.

The journey was unbearable. People were very thirsty and choking on the fumes from the chlorine. In every car, there were two SS men, one in the front and one in the back. In the first car there were only SS men.

When we stopped at Malkin, we all knew that we were headed for Treblinka. At the station, Poles were waving around a liter of water for sale. One of them said that we could have the water for 500 *zlotys*. I touched my belt remembering that I had 500 *zlotys* hidden there. I had been told that belts were not taken away from people and that having money on you was very important. I jumped at the chance to get the water and I readily gave the Pole my 500 *zlotys*. He showed me the water for a moment and then grabbed it away. He laughed cruelly and said that I was going to die anyway so I didn't need the water or the money. Some Poles were very cruel. The train started to move again on its way to Treblinka. The ride lasted maybe a day and a half with no food or water.

A big gate, covered with linen at the entrance to Treblinka prevented anyone from seeing anything inside. As soon as we exited from the train, men and women and children were separated. Women, children and elderly people went to the left and were taken inside. Younger men went to the right and stayed outside the gate. It was there that we saw an SS man, short and fat with red hair, standing with a big German shepherd dog, almost as big as him. You could see the man was mean just by looking at him. He said that he needed people to work. This was the only time during the operation of Treblinka, where 850,000 people were gassed, that men were taken out to work elsewhere. He asked who was a carpenter, shoemaker, barber etc. I lied and said that I was a carpenter. He was very mean and yet I will never forget him, for in the end he saved my life. He put his face close to mine, and said in German, "If anyone is lying about their skills, they will find out exactly what inside is." He walked up and down the line and asked everybody "*Vos bistu?*" (What are you?) And according to the answers picked 300 men; the rest of the people were sent to the gas chamber.

A regular train with seats was waiting to transport us somewhere. We could see Jewish clean up crews assigned to clean up the mess after the transport went inside. People had this job for a short period of time and then they were sent to the gas chamber and killed, and new people were taken from the next transports. Afterwards we found out that Himmler wanted to have it documented that not everyone who entered Treblinka was killed, and that was my luck. One of the men who was cleaning up with a broom said, as if talking to himself because we were not allowed to talk to each other, "You guys are lucky, you are going back to life. We will be killed soon and they will pick new workers to clean." He did not talk directly to me. He just kept on looking down. No direct conversation was possible. These people already knew what was inside.

Then they put us inside the train along with large sacks full of the clothing from the people who had been exterminated in Treblinka. An SS officer came onto the train with a bayonet and stabbed at the sacks to make sure that there were no people hiding in them. The train pulled out of the station and I breathed a temporary sigh of relief thinking we were on our way to work someplace. There were several work camps in the area including Czestochowa, Radom and Skarjis.

On the train we were able to communicate with each other. Everyone was numb, almost crazy in their minds. I was still feeling like I was the same Shulem and I was fighting to see what would be. After four hours, the train arrived at Lublin where we all got out. I figured that we were sent to Lublin because there were many factories in the area.

We started to walk, each line four people across with SS officers all around. The people from Lublin looked out of their windows; we could hear them saying to one another in Polish, but talking about us, "Go on, keep walking, you're walking to your death!" and they seemed to be happy. We just kept on walking and walking for over an hour, and then we saw the barracks of Majdanek. At the time we didn't know yet what Majdanek was but we found out very quickly.

The camp was divided into several sections, Feld I, II, III, IV and V. Feld I was right at the entrance of Majdanek. Feld II was mixed. Feld III was for Jews, the same as Feld IV. Feld V was just for women.

The people working there were the Slovaks who were mean.

They gave us some soft soap and took us to the shower to be cleaned. They took all of our valuables. Our own clothes were replaced with clothing from people who had been gassed. They left us our belts. We received a jacket and pants, but no underwear. The clothes may have been too big or too small, but you had to take what was given to you. If anyone complained, they were hit over the head by the Slovak. The clothes they gave me fit OK, unlike some others I saw. No socks were given and in place of shoes they gave us wooden clogs, the kind they wear in Holland. We had to stand in line while a soldier carrying a large pot of red paint painted the letters *KL* on the back of the clothing we were wearing. This stood for *konsentration lager* (concentration camp). After that we were assigned numbers, these were engraved on a piece of metal that we had to wear around our necks. I didn't know then what it all meant and what was going to happen.

The roads in the camp were made from keezel stones. The clogs soon started to rub against my skin and my feet started bleeding. Someone discovered that if you use the paper from the cement bags on your feet it would relieve some of the pain and bleeding. The Kapo of our commando caught a guy wearing the paper in his clogs and they beat him mercilessly. They warned him that he would be shot if he did it again. I had put newspapers in mine, but when I heard about the other guy I quickly took out the paper and threw it away. To this day, I have trouble with my feet.

We were immediately put into barracks. I was in barrack #22. I looked around for a bed; I was so tired from the recent days' events that I longed to sleep. "There's your bed!" The head of barrack 22 told me. He pointed to straw filled sacks on the floor. He was a Polish military prisoner and a Jew, a terrible man who had two strong henchmen working with him. They would wake people up in the morning and beat them up for no reason.

The following morning, after being woken up at five, we were put into 'Kommando' work groups which numbered around fifty people. We knew which group to join according to the numbers that had been assigned to us the day before. We were then told to file up by a long wooden trestle that stood out in the yard. Each one of us was given a red metal bowl containing black, bitter coffee made of *cikoria*. In Poland, *cikoria* was a poor

51

man's version of coffee. Usually you drank it with milk and sugar, which made it tolerable, but here there was no milk or sugar.

Things had not improved by lunchtime. Everybody got soup made from thistles. In Poland it was called *coltani*, or *Pokshiva*. It was chopped, cooked and looked similar to spinach. It tasted vile! We were all certain that the soup was made to make us sick and help us on our way to death. Everybody felt ill. Animals were fed better than we were. This "soup" gave everyone diarrhea, but if you needed to go the bathroom "out of turn" you were beaten with a shovel.

The bathrooms were outside of the blocks. Basically it was a big open hole surrounded by a board to sit on, and if someone gave you a push, you were likely to fall in and die. The smell was awful, and it smelled a mile away. From the soup, everyone needed to go.

After that, we were forced to march in and out, in and out just to drive us crazy. We marched until nightfall, and then we were given a piece of bread made from chestnuts. It was ground into a flour-like substance, and baked into bread. The bread felt heavy like clay, and not soft and light like regular bread. It was chewy like chewing gum. The trees that provided the nuts were called *Kashtanyen* trees. Most people only ate half the piece of bread and left half for the next day. It was by sheer willpower that I was able to stop myself from eating the whole piece of bread. Some were so hungry that they would steal from one another when they were sleeping, and then an argument would break out.

The next morning, everyone got up at five, and went to their Kommando Units. The Kapo was from

Dusseldorf, a German and a prisoner too. He was called The Dusseldorf Murderer; I heard that if anyone just looked at him the wrong way, their life was on the line. He was a giant of a man and looked very mean. Accompanied by the Kapo and one SS officer, we walked out the gate. They counted us walking out. Today, if I close my eyes I can still hear the tapping sound the clogs made as we walked over the stones.

We walked and walked until we arrived at a field. From where we were standing we could see a big hole with stones in the ground. Our clogs by this time had rubbed our feet sore; they were raw and bleeding. We were ordered to pick out large stones and take them to another hole. We went back and forth with the stones, taking them from one hole to another and then bringing them back again: useless and pointless work. The activity was just for show and to prove to the world that they weren't just killing people.

If anyone fell when carrying these heavy stones, the Kapo would take great pleasure in beating them about the head with the handle of a shovel. I made sure that I knew when he was coming, and then I tried to make it look as though I was working hard. Some people were not so lucky, everyday the Kapo made sure to kill at least four or five people. He would walk up to them from behind and hit them hard across the back of the head. If they didn't die instantly he would call one of his henchman over to finish the job.

Everyday was the same, and everyday when we finished hauling stones we walked back with the Kapo and the SS officer. We had to walk through a gate guarded by two SS men. It was their job to count the people, even the dead. The dead were carried back to the camp on shovels: two people held each shovel and the dead body would be put on the two shovels – legs on one shovel, head on the other. I was lucky and never got the job to help carry the dead bodies back to the camp. The count had to be the same as it was earlier in the day, when we left the camp.

When we came back to the camp on the fourth day of being in Majdanek, they gave us a piece of bread and margarine shaped like a cube, and the *cikoria* coffee. It was a really big deal for us.

I found myself becoming friendly with some of the people in my block. Sometimes, I cracked a joke and for a few precious moments we forgot about the cruel and ugly situation we were in. When we talked, we talked about today, never yesterday, but we also talked about what tomorrow might bring.

* * * * *

Early next morning we were taken to the same area as before to work. We saw women picking up little stones using a stretcher like device. Suddenly something unbelievable happened. From afar, I spotted Gittel! I felt so happy tears sprung to my eyes. I yelled out to her. "GITTEL!!!!!!!! SHULEM? *Vie biste*?" (Where are you?) was the answer. I felt like I had just seen an angel. When I returned to Schultz and everyone was gone from the bunker, I assumed all were dead, but here was Gittel - ALIVE! And she was supposed to be my future wife! "Where are you?" she called back. I told her I was in Feld 3, and she told me she was in Feld 5. I could not stop staring at this gorgeous girl with the beautiful green eyes. At Majdanek they didn't cut people's hair, so she still had her hair. "Catch!" she shouted, and threw me a piece of bread. "Where did you get the bread?" I asked her. "I saved half last night", she said. The women received better bread than the men.

The SS officer was looking at me as if I were crazy. Someone told him that I knew Gittel and that she was a relative. If they had known she was my girlfriend, she ran the risk of being exterminated.

After seeing Gittel, a feeling ran through my body: I MUST SURVIVE! Perhaps there was even the chance that I would find members of my family alive.

We came back to Feld 3 and I saw someone I knew from Schultz, who said he had some news for me. "Shulem," he said, "I saw your brother Monyek!" I couldn't believe my ears. "My brother Monyek? Where is he?" "He is in Feld 4. His Kommando was working together with our Kommando. I spoke to him and told him you were here." "I must see him," I said excitedly. "Monyek said that after your work tomorrow you should come to the barbed wire between Feld 3 and 4." One of the SS officers was looking straight at my friend, and he started to march over to him. "Can't talk," my friend said and walked hurriedly away, leaving the SS officer staring at him.

The next day, after our cup of *cikoria* and bread we had some 'free time' when we were allowed to circulate and talk amongst ourselves. I could not get to the dividing wire quickly enough.

Monyek and I were so happy to see one another. "Monyek!" "Shulem! *Vie bistu*?" I asked Monyek about our mother. He lowered his head and tears came to his eyes. For a moment he could not speak. And then he told me that she had suffocated in the cattle car from the fumes and tight quarters on the way to Majdanek, and they took out her body. Monyek went on to tell me that Edja, his wife, and their baby daughter had been taken to the crematorium.

Later, I found out that Gittel was also picked to go to the crematorium. Everyone was made to strip naked and then marched to the place where they would be gassed. As they huddled together, an SS officer came and stared at them up and down, gloating. And then he saw Gittel. "What's she doing here, she's not Jewish She doesn't belong here, she belongs with the other people", he said. She looked very non-Jewish with her blonde hair, green eyes and rosy cheeks. He chased her out and said "Get out, go back to the other showers." Gittel ran naked some 500 meters to the place where people were being sent to the real showers.

Word soon got out about Gittel and how she was going to be gassed and that she had been saved. The Polish women who took care of the showers and the block *Eldester* began saying that she came from heaven, "from the other world". It was unbelievable.

Chapter 7
Sol Silberzweig – No. 126622

In some of the local towns there were factories where slave laborers were making munitions and other products for the Germans. I heard from someone in Majdanek that people could register to go away to work. Gittel, Monyek and I all registered.

Several weeks passed and we didn't hear anything. In the meantime, everyday in the fields, people were being killed by the Kapos and their henchmen. Then one day, about three months after I was taken to Majdanek, from those who had registered, they picked the ones to be transported to work. Gittel, Monyek and I were all chosen. I just hoped that we were all going to be working together in a work camp like Czestochowa, Skarjis or Radom, and not a concentration camp. I hoped and prayed we would end up together.

We marched together and came to the train station in Lublin, along the same route we came into Majdanek. After a long wait a train arrived. Before we boarded, SS officers took their places along the track, and as we climbed inside the train they watched our every move. I was very happy to see that it was a regular train again and not a cattle train. I figured that maybe things were going to be OK. On the train, I was together with my brother; the women were in a separate car.

The train traveled for many hours. Finally it stopped. "OUT! OUT JEWS!" ordered the German soldiers, prodding us with their rifles. In the confusion Monyek and I became separated. Then suddenly I spotted him again. I called out, but he didn't hear me. An SS officer ran up to me and hit me on the side of my head with the butt of his rifle. "Bloody Jew!" he said in German.

I shuffled along with the others, hoping that I would make contact with Monyek. Then I saw Gittel among the women getting off their train, but I was not able to make contact with her.

The word spread quickly; we were in the worst place on Earth – **Birkenau**! The Germans had used deceit and lies again! They had given us false hope that we were being taken to work. All the while they were planning to take us to Birkenau. In Birkenau, a sub section of Auschwitz, there were six crematoria burning day and night.

* * * * * *

When I first arrived in Birkenau, I had no idea where I was. But at least I had my brother with me. I still had hope and would have as long as we stayed together.

Upon our arrival, the women went to the women's camp and the men were sent to the men's camp. First they took us to the delousing and the showers, and to change our clothes. We were slowly being dehumanized. At gunpoint we were forced into a line; a line that led to a place where we were all assigned numbers. The numbers were in the form of a tattoo! This was achieved by burning the skin on our arms with hot needles. I thought to myself, "What human being does this sort of thing to another human being?" When it came to my turn, I tried to think of other things, like the good times with my family, but the hot needles hurt too much and made it impossible to think of anything else. It took ten to fifteen very long and painful minutes to complete the tattoo. My number is 126622.

The men were assigned a six-digit number, and all in sequential order. Later there were also letters assigned for transport A or transport B. I thought at first that the tattoo was so that they could recognize you everywhere you went. But someone said that the tattooed numbers was the Germans' way of saying that there was no way to escape the number. A necklace number such as they gave us in Majdanek you could always throw away, and then escape or hide.

Together with a few other people, Monyek and I were put into a block. The first thing we noticed were the beds. In Auschwitz there were regular bunk beds. In Birkenau there were six people sleeping together in a bunk, three one way and three the other way. I was on the top bunk and Monyek on the bottom. There were no mattresses; we slept on a hard board. To cover ourselves we were given a thin blanket; one blanket for six people; everyone pulling at it, for a piece to keep warm. It was the Fall of 1943.

In the middle of the block was a sort of oven made from bricks; it kept the block *eldester* and his number two, the *shtub eldester* (they were Polish prisoners), warm, but did not do much for the rest of us. Holding a stick, the *shtub eldester* would walk around on the oven bricks in order to see everybody.

* * * * * *

59

A few hours after we arrived in Birkenau there was an announcement on the loud speaker calling for people to work in disinfection, ("*entlousing*" in German). " We are looking for people who have experience in disinfection of clothing." My brother didn't hear the announcement because had a hearing loss in one ear from the bombing of Warsaw. I told Monyek that they were calling for disinfectors and that I wanted to go to take a look. I was a bit of a smart aleck and I made it known that I had some previous experience with cleaning machines from home. They took my number and an hour later they called me to the front. They picked thirty-eight people out of thousands and I was one of them. They told us to go back and take our belongings. I came back and told Monyek I have to leave.

Before I left, I told Monyek that I would try to see him and try to help him. I told him that I would get something valuable and get it over to him. It was very hard for me to leave him; would he still be alive if and when I returned? We wanted to hug one another, but as usual the SS officers were watching. As the officer turned his back on us for a second, I kissed my brother goodbye and he cried, for he was sure he would never see me again.

The people who were working in disinfection were kept in a separate area from the main camp, so they could be close by when new transports came in and people needed to be disinfected. The small camp where I stayed was like a hotel compared to other parts of Birkenau. We had good clothes, showers and food: real food and not the kind of food we got in Majdanek. We got bread, salami and really tasty soup.

I was transferred to the delousing station. I was so surprised when I arrived at the new barracks, for the men were dressed in real clothes, there were real beds, real pillows, just like home. I could not believe it.

When I arrived at the delousing station, the Kapo, Moishe Chused started asking me who I was and where I came from. I told him I was the son of Yosel Silberzweig from Warsaw. It turned out that he was the son of the person who owned the cleaners on our street in Warsaw; he knew my family well.

Moishe gave instructions that no one was to touch me, that he knew my family from way back when and that I was part of the Warsaw ghetto uprising. I was pleased that no one was going to bother me. To know Moishe Chused was like knowing the President of the United States today!

All the people working in the delousing were already old timers at Birkenau. Their numbers were much lower than mine, only five digits. In the corner were big boxes filled with peoples' clothing. We had to search through all the clothes, the pockets, the lapels, etc. to take out everything we found and sort them into boxes. There were boxes for everything such as one for gold, one for money, one for diamonds, etc.

If anyone was caught stealing, it would mean certain death. After a few days I saw that some of the guys were taking things and hiding them so I decided to do the same. I took something small and hid it in my underwear. In this camp, people's heads were shaved, but they were allowed to wear regular clothes.

The people who came to Birkenau went through the disinfection, as well as other people who were sent to work in other camps. One of these places was "Yavozneh", a coal mine, another was Buna, a rubber factory, belonging to Auschwitz. They all went through our delousing first. One day I received a shock. Monyek was on one of these transports. "What are you doing here?" I asked him. His reply sent shivers up my spine. He was going to Yavozneh, the coal mine - a terrible place. People were sent to the mines inexperienced and were given no instructions. "You mustn't go there. I'll fix everything with Moishe," I cried. "He can fix it so that you won't have to go there!" I went to talk to Moishe. Moishe said to me, "Take him out or he will die there."

But Monyek refused to listen and said, "it is my fate to go there." "But people are dying like flies there," I tried to persuade him. I asked him again not to go, but he insisted. I gave him the bread and salami that Moishe had given me. It was a lot of food. I tried again to get him to stay with me, but he refused. This was the last time I saw my brother.

In my small camp, everyone was free to move around. It felt comfortable and not like being in a camp. I found out early on that the women's camp was close to where I was staying. One day I went to the wire that separated the two camps. I saw a girl that I knew from Warsaw, and I yelled to her to try to find Gittel and bring her to the gate.

When we had to go through people's personal belongings, we would find things like cigarettes, which could buy a half or whole loaf of bread. I told the girl that if she brought Gittel to me I would give her a whole pack of cigarettes; she could buy almost anything with a cigarette. She readily agreed.

I waited anxiously, pacing up and down. It seemed like an eternity until the girl returned… with my Gittel. Her head was shaved but I could see that she was still my Gittel! I spoke excitedly. I told her about my good fortune and the good place where I was working. She listened, not saying much. I could see that she was worn out, tired. "Catch!" I threw her a few packs of cigarettes. "You'll be able to get yourself some good things!"

I tried to see Gittel as often as I could, but it was far more difficult for her than it was for me. Gittel's Block *eldester* was a difficult person. When the transports arrived, the SS separated the women and children from the men, and the "Canada" Kommando people would go through the belongings of the new arrivals to take away. Gittel would trade the cigarettes for valuable stuff with the Canada girls.

The SS would make the selections – to the right meant life and the left meant death at the crematorium. Older people and women with children always went to the left. The screams when families were separated were something I have never forgotten. To this day when I see a mother with a child, I think of how it was when the boys were pulled from their mothers to join the men.

The people who went to disinfection lived. The others went to the crematorium. My unit was in charge of taking the clothes from the people going to the regular showers for disinfection. They were given towels and a bar of soap made from human fat. When we took their clothes, in return we gave them other clothes that had been disinfected earlier.

The transports arrived sometimes at a rate of one or two a day, and sometimes one or two a week. Often there were several hundred people arriving a day. They were loaded onto trucks and transported, not knowing where they were going.

Chapter 8
Typhus

I had been seeing Gittel quite regularly up to this point. Although separated by the barbed wire, our meetings made us forget for a while where we were. One day I was waiting as usual by the wire; Gittel did not come, and I was very worried. Was she alive or dead? Later that day I found out that she was sick with typhus. I was very concerned because many people were dying of typhus.

Gittel was in the hospital block. How could I get to see her? That was not easy. And then I thought, of course, Moishe, I would ask him to help me see her. Moishe came up with an idea: he set me up with a box of tools so I could go over there and say I was a plumber.

It was a life and death risk, but I had *chutzpah* (nerve). I told the guards at the gate that I needed to fix something in the hospital block. I had some cigarettes in the box hidden behind the tools. When I got to Gittel's block I gave the block *eldester* a pack of cigarettes and said, "While I'm here is it possible to look up a relative of mine?" As far as she was concerned I was a regular plumber visiting a sick relative.

She told me which bed Gittel was in and that she was feeling a bit better. If she knew Gittel was my girlfriend she could have made trouble for me.

Gittel almost fell out of bed with surprise when she saw me. It was wonderful to see her, although it was from a distance. I was afraid of catching the typhus.

Most people who had typhus were sent to the crematorium. The women working in the ward were very friendly with Gittel and when the guards conducted a selection in the sick ward, the women covered her with an extra straw mattress. I found out about this only later. All of this was sixty years ago, but I remember it as if it were yesterday.

I could not stay too long with Gittel as I did not want to arouse too much suspicion. I gave her two packs of cigarettes when no one was looking, and left. She did not stay much longer in the hospital. After she recuperated she was sent back to a regular block.

We continued meeting near the gate; the few stolen minutes we had together were wonderful. One day when we met, Gittel looked very down, her situation was terrible. The Polish women prisoners received mail and regular boxes with food delivered from home, including *chazer schmaltz* (pig fat), *grieven* (rendered chicken fat), chicken liver, etc. The Jewish prisoners no longer had homes, no longer had anyone to send them parcels. I gave her cigarettes to exchange for food with the Polish women. After she did this once or twice she started to feel more like herself again. We got one or two packs of cigarettes everyday because we were good workers. I shared them with Gittel and once she started to feel better she began to trade the cigarettes for gold pieces and gold rings with other girls from "Canada". All the things she got were small so she was able to hide them.

Life in my Kommando was comfortable for concentration camp life. We had blankets and pillows, and were able to shower everyday in the community shower. Then one day, the party was over! I felt very bad when I heard the news. I came down to earth with a heavy bump.

They sent all of the new people in the small camp back to the main camp. Even Moishe Chused couldn't help me this time. I was in this Kommando for only six weeks, but in that time I had managed to organize a couple of things to bring back with me. I came back to the main camp feeling very worried indeed.

Chapter 9
Yet Another Camp

One morning everyone was ordered to line up outside and strip naked. I never was able to get used to this humiliation. It was a very hot day and the sun was unbearable. We all stood there waiting, stripped not only of our clothes, but also our dignity. An open Mercedes drove up and stopped near us. Himmler had come to see the selection process. He stood up in the open car and just briefly glanced at the people who were standing there. He commented that these people looked too good in Birkenau. And then he prodded his driver in his back and they drove away. I was on the first line and saw this very clearly.

They put me into Block 20, a regular block. I was not a big shot anymore. I was put in the 101-*trupen lazaret* (troop hospital) to work for the German army. We made sewer canals outside the hospital to connect with the main sewer. It was tough work standing in the water. It was already October 1943, and it was damp and cold. We were happy when we finished working to come back to *cikoria* and soup, with a piece of bread. Some of the German officers were better than the others. They would throw pieces of bread at us. Others would throw cigarette butts and when prisoners would try to pick them up, the Germans would step on their hands with their boots and break them. My Kapo was a French Jew. I found out that some women were working not far away – and that Gittel was among them. The

Kapo was a nice guy and let me go see Gittel.

We still had not been given a uniform, just the regular clothes with a Jewish star on the front, which we wore with whatever pride we had left, and our number. The same number that was tattooed on the arm. On the back of our clothes, painted in red paint, was written KL, *Konsentration Lagger*. The Poles had a Polish star, the gays got a purple triangle, criminals had green and the black triangle was for people who were against the Reich – the political prisoners.

One morning when we marched to work, some SS men who stood by the gate picked out 8 to 10 people including me. "You go back to the block, you don't have to go to work today, they told us. This sounded very suspicious to me. We went back to the block and we thought that this was the end. People, who had sharpened the handles of their spoons like a knife, were giving them away, thinking they wouldn't need them anymore. Spoons were a rarity.

We all looked at one another. No one cried or even showed any emotion. After all, we were just a number. I figured it was just my luck.

It was early morning, still dark outside. The sun had not risen yet. Not that it ever seemed to rise in this hellhole. Everyone else had left for work. We tried to ask the block *eldester* what was going on, but he just yelled at us to shut up. An SS officer came with a book and said, "Let's go!"

It was about 5 AM, dark, raining, and cold. We were told to march ahead of him. As we neared the barracks of the gypsies we were told to stop in front of the barracks of some doctor called Mengele. "What are we doing here?" I thought. We didn't know who Mengele was at this point, or what he was doing. We thought he was a regular doctor and that he would take care of us. Little did I know that we were all there in the Mengele Laboratory to be castrated. They ordered me to strip completely; I was thankful that I didn't have anything like gold hidden on me at this time. I was told to put on a white apron. They pushed me roughly onto a stretcher and tied belts tightly around my feet and hands. They probably did the same to the others. "What the hell were they planning to do with me?" I thought. I was so afraid my body began to shake. Would I ever see my Gittel again? All of a sudden, an alarm went off; it was the first time it happened since I was in the camp. I could hear airplanes overhead and then bombs started to drop. Are they English planes? They could not be German. No, they had to be English or American.

Who would have thought then, that 60 years later, on September 4th 2003, Israeli Air Force F-15 jets would fly over that death camp sending a message to the world that, if Jewish lives anywhere in the world were threatened, the State of Israel would take the action that the Allied forces did not take in the 1940s.

The doctors did not hang around; they all ran away from Dr. Mengele's hospital, including Mengele himself, and left us alone. I started to wiggle back and forth until I managed to loosen the belts and free one hand. I did not wait around either. I put on my clothes and ran back to a different block (not my own) and I stayed there a few hours. Then when everything was quiet I snuck back to my block, first to the back of the block and from there I snuck up to my bunk. Now that I think about it, it is quite unbelievable. Again I survived a terrible fate. I never did find out what happened to the other people that were taken with me to Mengele.

There was a large wooden door at the rear of the block and every day when I looked out I could see the crematorium, with the smoke rising into the sky. The smell had a pungent sweetness... it was the smell of death, burning bodies. As the smoke wafted up into the sky, I imagined the shapes were of a man, a woman, a child... Under my breath I would say: I am still free!

* * * * * *

One morning as we went out to work at the *trupen lazaret*, trucks passed us filled with old people, women, and children; they were headed for the crematorium. They were saying: "*Shma Yisroel*. Take *nekama* (revenge) for us."

Before they went into the crematorium, people were given a piece of soap made from human fat, and a dark gray towel. This was another of the German deceits - trying to make the people believe they were going to take a shower.

After a few weeks of working in the sewers, I thought my good luck had run out. One day, when we were lining up to go to work, one of the SS officers pulled me out of the line with some others and dragged us to one side. "This is it," I thought. "I'm finished. I'm going to die." I closed my eyes and thought of Gittel. "Open your eyes, *Jude* fool! Unless you want to close them permanently." The officer laughed. We stayed behind in the Block and were certain that this was the end, we would be taken to the crematorium. Once again we gave away our spoons thinking we wouldn't need them anymore.

They put me and some 40 others on a truck and took us away. We didn't know where we were going. Along the way, we saw Polish people going about their daily lives. They were carrying cakes and geese and the smell was so good. I thought of their life and then I thought of mine. I felt sick with anger. After two hours on the truck, we reached a small camp.

It was bitterly cold when we arrived at this new camp. Winter had struck with a vengeance by dropping tons of heavy snow. Luckily, unlike other poor souls, I had an overcoat. I found out that the camp was in a town called Lagisha and that we were assigned to build machinery to produce electricity.

The next day, we discovered who was in charge of taking us to work, a Hungarian SS man named Schmidt, one of the worst murderers. On the way to the plant there was a hill with electricity wires. I heard that many people fell onto these high voltage wires and died. Not long after that, I learned that most of these people really had died at the hands of Schmidt. Every day at least four people died. Schmidt had two German shepherd dogs with him, trained to bite people's legs. The people who worked there said, "Wait and see how he gets his pleasure every day!"

The following day, people were passing out from the intense cold. Schmidt, the sadist, would run and push the dogs towards their legs. The dogs were well trained. Most people died either from his meanness or from falling down onto the wires. I was certain that the end of my life would be here.

I started looking around to see how I could get out of this terrible place. Another prisoner I befriended told me that a doctor named Stern was in a small hospital. "Talk to him", he said. I went to the hospital *Krainken Bau*. Dr. Stern was from Slovakia, and later I found out he was Jewish. I told the doctor that I had a pain in my ribs. I felt that I could talk to him.

"Here is a gold watch with a chain that my father gave me, please take it from me and try to save my life. I have a brother in Auschwitz and I would like to see him" (I lied – Monyek wasn't there anymore.) Stern agreed. "OK, Shulem" he said (that's how I found out he was Jewish), "this is what you do!" He told me to go to work the next day and slip down, then start to yell that I hurt my ribs. "Of course the Kapo will doubt your word and bring you to see me," he said. "I'll act like I don't know you, of course. I'll check you over and tell them that you have to go to the infirmary."

The next day, I did exactly what Stern told me to do. Schmidt fell for it hook, line and sinker. Soon I was lying in bed in a nice warm infirmary eating good soup with an extra piece of bread. I stayed there almost a week. Doctor Stern lived up to his side of the bargain; he had arranged for a hospital van to come from Auschwitz and take me and eight other people to the hospital in Auschwitz. This way the other eight people were rescued also because of me. Stern couldn't get a van just for me – one person. He was an angel. He risked his life. If they had found out what he did he would have been killed. People said that Auschwitz was a sanatorium compared to Lagisha.

(Years later at Yad Vashem I met Harold Hersch (who now lives in Atlanta), and told him that I had been in Lagisha. "So was I", he said. He worked in the kitchen, which was a good job because they had food. I told him that I was one of the eight that was taken in the van to Auschwitz. He said: "We were told that the eight were shot in the woods.")

After being in the hospital in Auschwitz a few days I was anxious to get out especially since I was really healthy. Another reason for me wanting to leave the hospital was that the SS came very often to the hospital to conduct selections. The very sick were sent to the crematoriums. I did not want to risk this, although there was better food in the hospital.

When I came out of the hospital I was given a striped uniform. It was the first time I had been given something other than regular clothing. When I left the hospital, I took some food with me.

I was sent to a block where the block *eldester* was a Jew from Belgium. I told him that I fought with the underground in the Warsaw Ghetto uprising, and he started to like me. I sat on the top bunk and my feet were hanging down. A voice said: "Take away your feet." The voice sounded familiar. I jumped down and saw a guy I knew very well from Warsaw and Praga, the same town as Gittel; his name was Shloyme Radoshinsky. We started talking and he told me that he was working in a potato cellar. "It's a good job," he said, " because you are inside and you do the work sitting down." "I would like to work there!" I said to him, "Can you do something for me?" " I'll try," he replied, "in the meantime, I have something for you." And he gave me a raw carrot and some other vegetables. "I'll take you with me tomorrow and I will talk to the Kapo and try to arrange to have you work in the same Kommando."

Shloyme spoke to the block *eldester* and asked him to let me go with his Kommando. Then he spoke with the Kapo. When the Kapo saw me - I was a *muselman* (skeleton) at the time – he took me to work in the potato cellar.

After a few weeks, they were looking for mechanics who knew how to handle machinery. I said I did, and so they sent me to a factory called Union. Here they made fuses for bombs, Fau-A and Fau-B they were called.

My work was making screws for the cylinders. There were three index machines making screws for the fuses. They had to have the wires inside and I made a lot of empties, to sabotage them. There was a lot of sawdust around to catch the oil from the machines. I used the sawdust to fill a lot of these empty screws. I made sure that the good screws were always on the top so that when the SS came around to check them, things always checked out OK. Once again, I tried to sabotage things at great risk to myself.

One day, the SS came to a Hungarian guy who accidentally made an error while making one of the screws. When the SS officer saw this, he took his rifle butt and beat him on his head and body until the guy was almost dead. I have never seen anything like it. His face was unrecognizable. It was so terrible it made me sick.

* * * * *

It was now 1944. I found out there were a lot of women being moved from Birkenau to Auschwitz to work in the Union factory to make plastics for the bombs. They built a women's camp in Auschwitz for these women. I had not seen Gittel for a long time at this point and missed her terribly. I made an arrangement with the female Kapo who was bringing the women from Birkenau to bring Gittel and I would give her a gift. A couple of days later, there she was, my beautiful Gittel.

Working in the screw section, I had access to pincers and wire cutters. The foreman of that section, Novack, a Pole who was not anti-Semitic, told me to put the wire cutters in the carpenters' shop. I did not query this, I just did as I was told. When I went to retrieve them the next day, they were gone. The foreman said he would arrange for new ones. Something funny was going on, but what, I did not know until later; the tools were being taken by the resistance. Had I known it was for the resistance, I would have done it earlier.

The main Kapo of Union was a German called Hans. His girlfriend Alma was a Kapo in the women's department, who liked Gittel. She told Hans not to bother me, and he didn't. (After the War, I found out he was stabbed to death by former prisoners.)

Out of all the Germans that I came in contact with, there was just one that sympathized with the people, a civilian by the name of Bishop. In the presence of the SS he gave the appearance of being tough, but when they were not around he was kind, talking to me and once even giving me half of his sandwich.

One morning planes flew over and began bombing

the area of Union which was an *abteilung*, (branch) of Krups, which made airplanes and tanks. We were not allowed to take cover, we just had to carry on as though nothing out of the ordinary was happening. The sound of the explosions was piercing and very frightening. Suddenly, Gittel came into my *abteilung*. She clung to me afraid. Thank goodness the SS officers at this point had run for cover and therefore did not see her. Tunnels holding the machine cables and covered with bricks were next to the machines. Novack moved two bricks out of the way and let Gittel and I, and some other people into this tunnel. This Kapo risked his own job by doing this. I asked him to join us, but he said he didn't care and whatever would be would be. After what seemed like an eternity, but in reality was about half an hour, the bombing stopped and we were all told to get back to work.

Several weeks passed, and one day we heard that they were going to liquidate the Union factory. We knew it had to be true because the Russians were very close.

One morning, we were all told to come together in the big field. There must have been thousands of people there. I looked around me, everyone looked worn out and broken. One of the SS officers shouted at us, and what he said was passed down the line. They were sending us back to Birkenau. Apparently there was more space there.

To add more to our misery, we learned that men and women were to be separated. "We'll hide in the barracks," I tried to convince Gittel. "They won't find us there!" But she refused. She was tired, drained of all will. "No, my darling," she said. "Whatever will be, will

78

be." And she returned to the women. I watched her as she went, and then I turned and went back to the men. It was impossible to know if I would ever see her again; I should have forced her to hide. Many people hid in Birkenau – Auschwitz, and were liberated by the Russians a few days later.

Chapter 10
Mauthausen and Dachau

It was January 17, 1945. After about fifteen months in Birkenau in groups of one hundred or so, we started the sixty-kilometer walk to the train station in Glawic. Our feet and hands were frozen from the cold. The rain and snow beat against our faces as we began the ten-hour trek. People dropped like flies along the way; the feeble and the weakest were the first to die. Our lives meant nothing to the Germans. To them we were not even human. Anyone who asked to relieve himself or herself during the march was shot. So we either had to hold it in or….

The snow crunched under our feet as we walked along the highway and through the woods. At some point they decided to stop along the way. The SS officers sat down to rest during this time, but nobody else was allowed to; we had to stand. Then, the order was given to start walking again. We dragged our weary bodies along; feet aching and souls almost destroyed. Another hour or so went by, and then the order came to stop. This time we were allowed to sit on the ground: the wet ground. All those hours without food and water, people were hungry and thirsty. Some took handfuls of snow to try and quench their thirst.

"Ok, on your feet, *fafluchte shvine* (dirty pigs!)" An SS officer shouted out. Broken and half dead, and with every ounce of energy that we had, we pulled ourselves to our feet and walked on. Finally we came to the train station in Glawic where we were loaded by the hundreds onto open cattle trains.

The train went through Pilzner, Czechoslovakia, where, as we passed under a bridge, the SS shot at some Czech people who were standing on the bridge throwing food baskets to us. I did not grab the food, but others did.

We traveled non-stop, standing up like pieces of wood, people relieving themselves in their clothes. The smell was awful. We were wondering all the while if we were being taken to another factory to work. We finally arrived at our destination, a place called Mauthausen - one of the worst camps that ever existed. The worst camp that anyone could imagine.

The human cargo was unloaded from the trains. Ten to fifteen people from each car had died en route from exhaustion and hunger. We had walked sixty kilometers, stood for hours in the freezing cold trains, and now they made us stand for hours in arctic-like temperatures, waiting to be counted. "Of course they don't care about us," I thought. "They don't see human beings before them, we're just numbers, and numbers don't have souls and feelings, so why should they show any pity towards us."

Hours went by, until eventually they allowed us to go into the block. No beds, no straw sacks, just a plain wooden floor. Everyone had to sit down next to each other in long lines; each one was sitting with their legs spread, squeezed into the next person. Unable to lie down or even move, many people passed out.

Those who were able, fell asleep leaning on one another.

At five o'clock the following morning we were awoken. "OUT, OUT, GET UP. *AUFSHTEIN, JUDE AROUSE*!!" After sitting in one position the whole night it was hard to move, we also had no strength because we had not eaten anything in two days. And of course no one had washed. We were sent back out into the brutally cold weather to be counted. Evening came and still we had only the hard floor to rest our sore bodies. By now they fed us a little soup and a piece of bread.

One or two days passed and I heard of people being taken to a place called Guzen. The Germans wanted to build factories in the mountains there, so stones needed to be removed; everyday hundreds of people went up there to remove stones. I had not been taken yet. On the third day I noticed that a block *eldester*, a non-Jewish Austrian, was wearing gloves with one finger made from lambskin. I took my life in my hands, and told him that I could make him the best pair of gloves that he had ever seen.

"I come from four generations in the fur business and I know how to make fur gloves. If you don't like the gloves, you can have me beaten," I said. I do not know where I got the guts to say that, but I did. The block eldester responded: "*Fufluchte Jude*, go away." But later he called me back: "Come here! What do you need to make the gloves?" I told him. They brought me a vest, needles, a thimble, some colored thread. "And I need a couple of pieces of old bread to clean the vest," I told them. Now, I was being a big shot, pushing my luck! I asked the block *eldester* to get me a piece of paper and a drawing of the form of his hand. It was amazing; they gave me everything I asked for.

In the block there were no beds, except in the corner where there was one double bed. The *stuber eldester*, a Ukrainian, slept on the bottom and the top was empty. The block *eldester* put me on the top. That's where I worked by day and slept at night. I was the only one that was allowed to sleep in a bed; I felt bad about that but I had to think of myself. The block *eldester* told the *stuber eldester* that I did not need to go outside to work or to be counted; I should be counted inside.

The next day the weather was very overcast, it was difficult to see what I was sewing, so I stood by the window for more light. What I saw made my blood run cold. In the freezing cold, people were made to remove their clothes and then, dipping them into a large steel basin containing bleach and squeezing out the excess water, put their clothes back on. They were then sent back inside, their clothes dripping wet. The Germans were here to murder our people; after all, anyone who did something bad to the Jews was wonderful. Who was going to tell them differently? I moved away from the window and went back to sewing the gloves.

Every night one or two people in each block died. They brought the bodies outside to a little wagon and took them down to the crematorium. All the time this was going on I continued making the gloves. It took me another four or five days, but eventually they were ready. I examined the gloves carefully to make sure they were perfect. I was worried that if there was anything wrong with them, the block *eldester* would punish me.

I showed the gloves to the block *eldester*, anxious for his reaction. I shook in my shoes as he looked at them. He called another guy. "Hanz, come here. *Zeymal vas the jude hot gemacht*? (See what the Jew made me?) He worked for days to make me these handmade gloves. *Gib* (give) him a *ganse brod*, a whole bread. *Gib* him *aine ganse folle shissel mit soupe.*" Inside the soup were pieces of meat and *grouven* and fat. I hadn't seen such food in years since I was taken to the camps. I had bread. I was a rich man.

The *eldester* asked me if I could make more gloves and I said yes. He gave me everything he thought I needed and then he asked if I need anything else. I thought of the other people suffering, and me living so well under the circumstances. So with the *chutzpah* that I had plenty of, I told him that I needed two people to help me with the sewing. I waited for him to yell and curse me, but he told me to go and pick out two people. I could not believe my ears. I quickly dropped my sewing and ran and grabbed two people, one of whom I knew from Auschwitz. Soon we were all sitting on the straw mattress sewing! The *eldester* brought vests and the materials I needed. The two men were sewing and I, at this point, became the cutter! The two men told me they would never forget me and that I saved their lives.

"We don't have to go out into the freezing cold anymore," they said.

A few days later we were still working on the gloves, when we heard that the Russians were near. The SS officers and soldiers were running around, gathering everyone and everything in order to clear the camp as quickly as possible. I had to leave everything. Soon, we were all on the move once again, marching down the mountain to the town and on to the train station.

An open train was waiting for us. As they loaded us

into the train, people in the street were saying among themselves in a very anti-Semitic way, loud enough for us to hear, how we were going to our slaughter "the *yuden geyen aun hofen*" (the Jews are going to the garbage dump). They showed no mercy whatsoever. I had spent two months in Mauthausen, February to April and now we were traveling somewhere else. We did not know where.

The train came to a stop at Dachau; camp Dachau is in Germany near Munich. We did not know anything about this place, but we soon found out. Later, we discovered the truth about all the people who had been killed in Dachau, and about their mass graves.

The blocks were all right at Dachau; beds for everyone, bunk beds, up and down. We had been there a short time, when one of the SS officers said they needed someone to work in the disinfection section. As usual, I volunteered and said I had already worked in such an area in Birkenau. He seemed satisfied with that, and told me that I was to be the foreman and to pick ten others, and to report the next morning. Mostly the items to be disinfected were uniforms of the German SS. We took the opportunity and looked through the pockets, sometimes we were lucky and found cigarettes.

All of a sudden an order came; everyone, Jews and Poles should come to *appel platz* – a large field. I tried to hide but the Poles told me, "Go, they need you over there." When we arrived, we were told that all the Jews were being sent to Switzerland to be exchanged for German soldiers. We were being traded for German soldiers! German soldiers were coming to Germany and we were going to Switzerland. We heard it, but we did not believe it. Was it another one of their lies, deceiving us yet again?

Something else happened in the field, which was really hard to believe; we were given Red Cross packages. Chocolate, crackers, cans with meat, some cigarettes, all this was lying around in the camps in their original packaging sealed up for years in warehouses and had never been given to the prisoners! We all started to grab at the packages, hardly daring to believe our eyes. Some people ate and others waited, because we never knew what would come later. It was very suspicious. Some Jews hid in the blocks and the gentiles did not give them away. These were Czechs or other nationalities, not usually Poles.

Then they put us in regular trains with seats. It was wonderful. Even with the SS in the front and the back, we began to think that maybe they were telling us the truth! The train began to move slowly and then picked up speed, past German houses and towns, going, going, going…

As night fell, the train pulled into a station just outside the village of Innsbruck, Austria – now under German occupation. The SS started shouting for everyone to get out. Apparently we had arrived in a farming village; we were going to spend the remainder of the night in barns.

Early the following morning, we awoke to gray skies, everyone thought that we were going back to the train to complete our journey, but that was not to be. I noticed that some of the people were missing; they had run away during the night.

We started to walk and walk and walk, a pathway

leading us into the woods. As we were walking in the woods, people asked for permission to go to the bathroom in the woods. The German soldiers gave their permission, and as the prisoners walked into the woods the Germans shot and killed them. We realized that the story about Switzerland was a lie and that the Germans had tricked us yet again and were going to kill us.

Suddenly from out of nowhere it seemed, a motorcycle with two SS, one an officer, appeared out of the woods, headed towards us, and stopped. The officer shouted to our German 'escorts', "Halt! Where are you going? You have to go back to Innsbruck, the enemy is over there." We turned around and began to walk back. Everyone walked in silence, all with one thought - that we had been cheated out of our freedom and were being sent back.

It was only later that we found out that the officer we encountered was not the SS, but an underground member impersonating an SS officer. They saved the whole transport. A bit further down in the woods, there were big ditches filled with bleach. The SS were planning on shooting everyone and leaving us for dead in the forest. Of course we thought we were being cheated out of our freedom, but in fact we were being saved from our death. Again – I survived with my life!

We were back on the open train and heading from Innsbruck through the mountains towards Mittenwald. There they marched us all, hundreds of people, to a huge valley filled with water. It was the end of April, and the water from the melting snows on top of the mountains surrounding us, was running down into the valley, which was slowly filling up with water. Night was falling and the freezing water was almost up to our knees. (I still suffer with my knees until this very day.) Young and old, all of us blue with cold. It was terrible. How much more were we expected to endure?

There was no moon that night and it seemed as though darkness fell all of a sudden. The silhouettes of the SS standing around with their machine guns could just be made out. Then suddenly, I saw the senior officer with his girlfriend and they appeared to be arguing. I could hear her saying that they were going to kill everybody, and that her family was in Mittenwald and if something went wrong, someone would end up killing her family in town to take revenge. And then the two of them drove away in their car. This probably saved me again.

The air was still, and then a light snow started to fall. The outlines of the SS faded and as the snow fell heavier, they could not be seen at all. I noticed that some people were missing, disappeared. "What's the matter with you, Shulem?" I asked myself. "What are you waiting for, do something!" I started to crawl on my belly like an alligator to the top of the valley up above to a little hill, and a highway, which led through the mountains. As I crawled across the highway, SS started shooting at me, and at others who tried to escape, their shots probably missing because of the snow. In front of me lay the mountains, tall and wide. I stopped for a moment to stare at them wondering how I was ever going to climb them. And then I felt some strange power come over me as if I were given a transfusion of strength. I began to walk higher and higher and higher; I did not even know where I was going.

Suddenly, in the distance I could hear people speaking Yiddish. Who would be speaking Yiddish? Polish Jews? I walked cautiously forward and saw them, about six people sitting in a big hole covered with branches from evergreen trees. I came out into the open where they could see me. It was then I saw that one of them was a friend of mine from Bialystok. "Shulem'ke!" He said, pleased to see me. "Come here, come here."

They could not offer me any food, as they had none. All they had to eat was snow. We sat around talking for some time and then we fell asleep. In the distance we heard the sound of bombing.

As daylight broke, we awoke to see a young man walking towards us. We waited until he got closer and then we grabbed him. "Who are you, what are you doing here?" we asked roughly. The man was quiet for a moment and then started rambling nervously in Polish. "Could be a German pretending to be a Pole." my friend from Bialystok said, "We'll tie him up and put him in the hole before we decide what to do with him!"

First, we checked his pockets, but he had nothing except a lighter. This was quite a find! We put snow into some rusty old army cans that we found lying around, and used the lighter to melt it until it became water. As we all took a sip I thought that champagne could not have tasted nicer. It was wonderful, a *mechaye*! (pleasure).

On the third day of sitting around in the hole, we noticed that the bombing had stopped. We still had the Pole tied up to make sure he did not run away and tell the Germans of our whereabouts.

"One of us must go down the mountain to see if it's

safe for the rest of us to go down," I said. Up to now I had not really spoken much. "If we stay up here much longer we'll die." And so it was agreed, we would draw for it. We tied a knot in a piece of rag and the one who pulled out the part with the knot – lost. A young man lost the draw and went down; our lives were in his hands. We told him that he must come back up to tell us what was going on – otherwise if something happend to us it would be on his conscience.

It was some time before we heard him yell up to us, "COME DOWN, *Ingalach*, (young men) different people are here – not the same! There are no more Germans!" There was an echo, and then we heard him again. "I see other people in cars and trucks with a star. I don't know who or what they are, but they're not Germans." When we heard this, we untied the Pole and began to make our way down the treacherous mountain.

Coming down off the mountain I could make out the jeeps with the star, a white star. The Russians also had a star on their jeeps. Then I heard a language being spoken, which was not Russian. It was a language that I knew slightly. It was English!

Suddenly, I forgot that I was starving, with very little energy, and I began to run down the mountainside. The soldiers in their jeeps stared up as I almost collided with them at the bottom. Right in front of me, stood an American commander. I was so happy to see him I fell on the ground, grabbed his feet and cried. At that point I must have passed out for when I came to, he was trying to revive me with some cognac. He probably saw the number on my arm. He told me in broken Yiddish that he was Jewish and that his name was Colonel Stern. After everything I had been through the first person I saw was a Jew! He told me that they were the 1st Army division and that they had come from Italy, through Austria to Germany. He looked intensely at the living skeleton that was before him; I weighed about 100 pounds and was filthy from going around for days and days. Colonel Stern told the soldiers to take me to the mobile hospital they had with them. "Don't worry fella," he said kindly, "you're gonna get washed and fed. We'll talk later and you can tell me all about yourself and where you came from."

In the hospital they immediately gave me something to eat, whole boxes of food. I cried with happiness. Then they washed me and gave me a brand new American uniform complete with shoes and a wool hat. Also I made friends with one of the soldiers, an American Pole; we were able to communicate in Polish. Whatever I wanted to say he translated for me.

I found out later, that the other guys who were with me in the mountains had run in the opposite direction, so I do not know to this day what happened to them. I was allowed to rest, and some time later, Colonel Stern came to see me. With my limited English and his broken Yiddish somehow we managed to communicate. Gradually I told him of the horrific ordeal that I and the other Jews had endured. I also told him about my brother Yacob (Jack) Silberzweig who left Berlin in 1939 and went to live in New York. Col. Stern made a note of it.

Sol after liberation

Chapter 11
Revenge

In the beginning it became a *rache*, a *neckama*, revenge against the Germans. The Americans announced on loud speakers in English and German: "Come down from the mountains. If you don't come you will be shot." The Germans heard and came down. I was told that I could go and help round up those Germans who had run away. Apparently a lot of them had been seen in the mountains, the same mountains where I had been. We were so lucky; if they had spotted us they would have shot us, or taken us for hostages.

When we came upon an SS hiding in the mountains, we discovered that he had taken off his epaulet to disguise the fact that he was SS. I asked him in German, "What are you?" His reply was that he was a soldier. I asked why he took off his epaulet. He did not reply, so I asked him to take off his shirt. A tattoo was clearly revealed. In Dachau I saw an SS officer with the same SS tattoo in his armpit when he changed his clothes. That proved he was SS. "You dirty dog," I shouted at him, the anger that had been suppressed for so long now boiling inside me. "Why didn't you tell me you were SS!" I slapped him in the face. It felt so good. The American Pole told me to do it again and again. I told the Polish American about the showers in Dachau where I first saw an SS officer with the same tattoo in the armpit. That is how I knew about it. After this the Americans gave me the authority to check the German prisoners for tattoos. Ten to twelve SS tried to pull the wool over my eyes by telling me they were not SS, just a soldier, a *vermacht*. I got mad at one of them for lying. I took him over to a little hanging rope bridge and made him walk to the middle. The Americans shook it hard and he fell to his knees. "Revenge is so sweet," I said, and I shot him. He fell into the water and floated away. Before the *rache* (revenge - German) was over I had shot several SS – this was just the first *neckama* (revenge - Hebrew).

It was an unbelievable feeling. After years of being a prisoner – now with a gun in my hand I could take revenge!

There were a couple of small farmhouses belonging to local farmers, where the Americans were staying. They took me to one of these farmhouses where a German family was living. Stern brought along a guy who spoke German. He told the farmer to take me in and give me a nice room, a bed to sleep in and a place to wash. He also told them to take good care of me or they would suffer.

The family treated me very well, and for the first time in years I slept in a bed with pillows and covers. It was like heaven. The first morning that I was there the daughter, a pretty young woman, served me breakfast in bed. She stayed a while as I ate, flirting with me. I would gladly have taken her there and then, but I was concerned about her husband. One afternoon, as I was bathing she slipped into the room and tried to seduce me. I certainly did not resist. I had not held a woman in years. She opened her blouse and drew my head to her breast. In that brief moment, I suddenly felt human again. We made love: warm passionate love, and it felt good after all those years. I gave her some chocolate and cigarettes (I had plenty of boxes from the soldiers who took pity on me.)

Later I went down to eat with the whole family. I did not give them any information and nobody asked me any questions. They were too afraid.

That evening Col. Stern came to me, together with a Jewish guy from Brooklyn, who spoke Yiddish. He told me that the Army would soon be moving along and that I should stay there. "There will soon be a Military Governor of Garmisch," he said, "perhaps you would like to work for them!"

I remained with these German people. The house was on the highway, the same place where I ran away. I found out later that the Germans killed 300 people in the valley. They had shot them. Had I not run away, I would have been dead too. Later, I went back and visited a cemetery where the 300 victims were buried.

Two houses down from the house I was staying at was a house owned by a fat woman with a red face named Frau Shmuker. Apparently when Hitler came to Mittenwald he had stayed at her house. I was told that she worked with the Nazis and was even one herself. One day I introduced myself to her and she asked who I was. I told her that I was a former prisoner. She acted like she was sorry, but I got the feeling that she was not. I found out that this area, referred to as Bertesgardens, was home to many Nazis.

A couple of days later I found out that a former German army camp in Mittenwald had been converted into a camp for the escaped prisoners who came out of the woods and were now free.

As soon as I could, I went down to the Military Governor in Garmisch and told him that Colonel Stern of the 1st Army had freed me, and that I would like to take revenge on the Germans for what they did to my family. I told him my name and showed him my ID which I received in the camp.

He asked me if I was interested in working with the Military Government. When I told him that I was, he said he would think it over and let me know. Many people who were freed went into the black market business, but I just wanted to work with the Military Government. Not long after our conversation, the Military Governor sent an MP with a jeep to pick me up in Mittenwald to bring me to Garmisch. There was no waiting around, he saw me almost immediately. "OK," he said. "You are going to be working with me!" (He was probably in touch with Col. Stern.)

Part of my work was to find out who committed wrongdoings, so it occurred to me to start talking with Post Office workers and train conductors. I thought if anyone had information to divulge they would. First I became friendly towards them; giving them nice things like chocolate, coffee and cigarettes, which were most important to them, and then I gradually started to ask questions. "Do you know what happened during Hitler's time?" Right away I could tell that these people had not been involved with the Nazis, but they did have some interesting information to disclose. In Mittenwald there was a hill covered with grass. Near the hill there was a telephone generator and near it, under the grass, were steel doors. They told me to open the doors.

I immediately contacted the governor, telling him to send some armed people because I had some important information. Within no time, two jeeps and a number of Military Police arrived. Together we went to the spot. Hidden behind a large patch of grass was a steel door. The door led to a passageway that went at least half a mile into the mountainside, to a warehouse as big as a football field stocked with goodies from all over the world: boxes of meat, coffee, chocolate, cigarettes, cheeses, champagne, wine, liquors and more, as far as the eye could see. For a moment we just stood and stared at this Aladdin's cave. I told them there was a DP (Displaced Persons) camp nearby and the people could use some of these good treats. One of the MPs shook my hand. "Good man!"

It took several days to move everything out. The food was sent to the camp, but the army took all the alcohol. This was my first find and the Military Governor congratulated me. When I came into the camp with the food, some of my former prisoner friends saw me and shouted "Shulem." They saw that I was already working with the Americans.

Every day a jeep was sent to pick me up at the German house where I was still staying; I imagined they thought I must be important, working with the Military Government. One day I had a message to go to the postman, he had something important to tell me. I arrived at his place with a gift for him, which made him very pleased. He told me that during the war several parachutists came down in the area and that farmers living in a nearby house killed them with stones and sticks. "Go to this house," the postman said, "and upstairs the attic has a double floor, there you'll find machine guns, the vests, and shoes of the parachutists which the farmer hid."

When I came to this house with MPs, I asked the farmer if he had anything upstairs and he said no. When we went upstairs with the tools, he started shaking. We ripped up the floor in the attic and there hidden under straw we found the guns, vests and shoes just as the postman had said. The farmer and his family claimed they knew nothing about it. I beat them up. We took the whole family to the military governor and told him everything. They were put in jail.

I received another tip about a house, where they said several machine guns were hidden in the kitchen under big piles of coal. When we came to the house and saw the coal, we asked the owners why they were keeping the coal inside the house. They replied that they kept it there to prevent it getting wet from the snow or rain. We started digging in the coal and found three machine guns.

I asked the woman of the house why she lied to us and she said she didn't know who brought the guns. I went upstairs to look around, to see if I could find anything else, and saw drawers filled with pictures. Pictures of how Jewish people were killed; the people in the pictures were naked and they were shot in the head. The woman denied knowing anything about it. "My husband did it. He is now a prisoner in Russia." "Was he an SS?" "Yes", she said. I kept the pictures for over fifty years and now they are in the care of Yad Vashem and will be in their new Museum.

We took the people from the house, placed them

under arrest and closed the house. They were later sent to jail for possession of weapons. There had previously been an order issued when the Americans took over, that people had to turn in all their munitions.

Back in Mittenwald, the townspeople were already talking about how the *Jude* living with the German people was working with the Military Government. They started to be unpleasant to me. They did not know that I was working with the post and train people!

There and then, I made up my mind to go and look for my family, and for Gittel. Someone told me about a very big DP camp nearby in a town called Feldorfink, which would be a good place to start. So I headed there loaded with food to be divided and handed out in the men's and women's camps.

When I arrived, my first impression was how huge the camp was; there were so many people. Everywhere people who knew me were calling out to me. I decided to go first to the women's camp on the chance that I might find Gittel. A girl named Dora claimed to know Gittel Rosen very well. They used to live on the same street in Warsaw Praga. (Dora now lives in Israel). Dora and another girl suggested that I come and live in Turkheim; it was a very nice place and I could do similar work from there. The two girls shared a house there. I thought it over and decided to go. Besides, I didn't want to live anymore in the little town of Mittenwald, I wanted to live where there were more Jews.

I told the Military Governor in Garmisch that I wanted to move away from Mittenwald, that it was a constant reminder of the place I escaped from. He advised me to go to another Military Governor in a different town, perhaps Mindelheim, and maybe work for them.

The German family was sad to see me go; they had become used to me giving them gifts. I met up with Dora and her friend again and accepted their invitation to stay a few days with them in Turkheim. In the evenings Dora and I would talk. I told her how I was searching for Gittel and when I found her I would marry her. I sensed that Dora, a pretty girl, was jealous. Dressed in the civilian clothes that the Americans had given me, I went and introduced myself to the Military Governor in Mindelheim, but it seemed he already knew all about me. I was given a permit to the Berger Meister, the mayor, and he gave me a nice house to live in.

One day, I went to Feldorfink and was very upset that the Jewish people there, after all they had been through during the war, were still living in camp conditions. I went straight back to the Military Governor and told him of my findings. He appointed me head of housing in Turkheim enabling me to help the people coming out of the camps (later I also arranged permits for Jews coming out of Russia). The following day I went back to the camp with Dora. I saw someone there who ended up being the chief of police of Tel Aviv, Motek Perlmutter and also two friends of mine, Shloyme Radoshinsky and Salek Olivek. I told them to pack up everything they had and come with me.

I found rooms in German houses for them, although the Germans hated having Jews living with them, but they knew that if they objected, I could easily have them removed from their homes. Actually, I did throw some

Germans out of their houses and put a couple of my friends there. I felt like I was taking my revenge out on them, and it felt good. When it became known how I was helping people, new arrivals started to come to me and I would set them up.

Two weeks after being in Turkheim I wanted to move to a nicer house, the house of Bergman, a Nazi and school director. It became known to me that Bergman had terrorized the school children during the War - questioning them about the activities of their parents. "Do people come to your house? Do you have meetings in your house?" He was trying to find out about anti-Nazi activity. When I discovered that he had beaten children to get information from them, I threw him and his wife out of their house. What a beautiful house it was too! When Mrs. Bergman started to cry, I told her how the Germans had thrown me out of my house and took away my business, which had been in my family for four generations. Without any pity for her and her husband I told them to pack their bags and leave.

Motek Perlmutter and Dora moved in with me, Dora doing her best to make me fall in love with her. I saw Perlmutter a couple of times after the war and later in Israel. His son was killed during the Six Day War.

By this time I owned my own car, a Citroen. Someone told me that up in the hills in the woods Nazis were hiding in a big house. I drove up there with Motek as my assistant working with the Military Governor. What we found were not Nazis but something else.

We arrived at the house to find a woman living there. When I told her that I was from the Military Government from Mindelheim, she looked nervously towards the curtains and began to shake. I walked cautiously over and pulled the curtains apart. There, piled up in front of me were about 500 rolls of material; the kind of stuff that was used for German SS uniforms. When I questioned her I told her the material now belonged to the Military Government.

We loaded up the whole car full of the materials and made our way back down to Turkheim. There I gave away several rolls of fabric to the head of the Jewish Komitet telling him that it was intended for the poor people who did not have any clothes. The rest I took to my house. Fabric was a very rare thing and could be traded for almost anything. The front of the guesthouse called "Crowne" was used for the Komitet meetings. The owner of "Crowne" was one of the biggest Nazis in town.

* * * * * *

I wanted to look for Gittel, and found out that a friend of hers Monyek Guss (another person with the same name as my brother in law) lived in Landsberg. He was a furrier I knew before the War who used to live in Praga and he knew Gittel.

It was during a trip to Landsberg, about fifteen kilometers from Turkheim that I met up with Monyek Guss. I immediately asked about Gittel. "Had she survived?" He told me she had and that he had seen her. "She returned to Warsaw to see if she could find someone in her family."

I remembered the agreement that Gittel and I made to each other; it was on the 18th of January, when they liquidated Auschwitz. We agreed that if we both survived we were to meet each other in Praga.

Monyek Guss went on to tell me how, after the war, around April or May 1945 he had seen Gittel on the Russian side of Germany, East Germany, outside Buchenwald. She was in Buchenwald when the Americans liberated the camp and she remained there even when the Americans left and the Russians took over. Monyek went with the Americans but Gittel had told him that she was going to Praga; she had a date to meet me. Her family had been gassed in Treblinka and she already knew that.

When I met up with Monyek, it had been only a couple of months since he had seen Gittel. I suddenly had a feeling of hope! Maybe she was still in Praga. I was very anxious to find her.

A lot of my friends at that time were making *aliyah* (immigrating) to Israel. I belonged to the *Aliyah Bet* organization, organizing money to help smuggle people into Israel via Austria. Motek wanted to go to Israel to be with his neighbor from Plonsk, Poland, David Ben Gurion. He told me I should go too. But I had other plans: to find Gittel.

Chapter 12
The Search for Gittel, and
Back in Business

I went to Warsaw by a cattle train. There were no regular trains going to Warsaw at this time. We arrived at Praga by train. How strange everything looked. Most of the place was in ruins. I made my way to the restaurant at Pjeska 18, where Gittel and I had agreed to meet. It was next door to Gittel's family's shoe store. The owners of the restaurant were two sisters who knew me as a nice looking boy who used to come to see the Rosen girl. They were happy to see that I had survived. I asked if anyone from the Rosen family had came back after the war. They said Gittel had stopped by to say hello, but then she went away.

I was walking around, remembering things as they once were. I was told to go to the Jewish Komitet where people who looked for family wrote their names on the wall.

All of a sudden, I saw a friend of Gittel's, Hannah, who was her neighbor. "She was here asking for you," Hannah said. "Gittel signed her name on the wall." "Where did she go?" I asked. "Lodz, to look for you!" It was then my mind went back to 23 Nowolipie Street. I remembered that we had buried a safe under the ground in the cellar. We were rich people before the war. There was a lot of gold, dollars, diamonds…. My brother put it there to be used by whoever lived through the war. I told Hannah about the safe and thought maybe I should take someone with me to go there. She warned me off. "The AK, Army Krayova, will follow you wherever you go, they're very anti-Semitic. They follow survivors, see where they're digging, shoot them on the spot and steal whatever they had."

The AK was made up of former Polish army people and they were murderers. So, I decided to give up the safe, and go to Lodz, thinking maybe Gittel would be there.

Like a lost person I wandered around searching for Gittel. Obviously there were no telephones or other means of communication at the time, and it was very difficult to find someone. Then, I made up my mind to return to Turkheim; it had been a few weeks since I left. I was going back without Gittel. But at least I knew she was alive.

The journey back to Germany was a very unpleasant experience. I did not travel on a regular train and the passengers, mainly Poles, were stealing from other passengers. After an exhausting two days of traveling I finally arrived back in Turkheim.

It continued to bother me that I could not find Gittel. I had to go to Poland and try again, I had to find her. I packed some things that I thought I could use to trade, such as fine leather, silk and some nice fabric, and then I was off again.

Once again I traveled on a cattle train. There were no seats, so we had to sit on the floor. Many people were stealing from each other. It was terrible. I sat in the corner and tried to protect my things. I tied my suitcase with string to my arm.

I went to Lodz and walked around. Then I went to

Reichenbach, a town that used to belong to Germany and now belonged to Poland, where many refugees had settled. After two weeks I again came back to Turkheim empty handed.

On a trip to Landsberg, I spoke with a girl who had worked in the Union factory in Auschwitz. I told her "If you find where Gittel is, I will give you a gold watch." One morning someone woke me up shouting, "Shulem, I have good news for you – I know where Gittel is!"

It was the girl from Union. She told me that while on a train going to Frankfurt she had met a man. He introduced himself and then they started talking about the war. It seemed that they had places and names in common, and before long the man mentioned the name Shulem, and that he knew where Shulem's girlfriend was. He wrote down his name and address on a piece of paper and told the girl to give it to me. "Here it is," said the girl and handed me the piece of paper. The name was Alex Porzitcki and the address was in Marburg, a day's train journey away.

Sitting on the train the next morning, I thought to myself, "Now I am a big shot, Nazis are afraid of me, and yet just a short while ago I was a prisoner in a concentration camp!"

After changing trains in Frankfurt, I finally arrived in Marburg. Alex's address was not difficult to find and soon I found myself at his front door; he lived on the first floor in a German house, with his sister.

He made me most welcome. "Come in, I've heard so much about you. Would you like to rest after your journey? Are you hungry?"

All I wanted from this man was information about Gittel. He smiled at my obvious impatience. "Sit down and I'll tell you what I know about Gittel Rosen." And then Alex began his account of what he knew about Gittel.

"It was a couple of days after the war had ended. A friend of mine, David Santzer, and I were together in the DP camp in Buchenwald. One morning David went out into the street towards the train station. The camp was mostly for men so he was surprised to see a girl sitting on the bench; she looked like a *shikseh* with her blonde hair and green eyes. As he walked over to her he saw that she was barefoot and dirty, her dress torn and stained, her hair uncared for and her broken nails caked with dirt. He sat down beside her and started talking to her. She told him that she had just walked out of the woods after she ran away from a death march. Apparently, the Germans guarding her and the other Jews, finding out that the war had ended, ran away and left them.

David tried not to stare at her, but he noticed a Jewish star that she had been wearing around her neck fall out of her dress. "Are you a *yiddishe maidel*?" he asked her. She nodded her head.

"David's heart went out to her; he put his arm around her and took her back with him to the DP camp. He arranged for her to have a room where she could rest. "Here's soap, clean pants and a shirt, make yourself at home," he told her, and went off to town to organize dresses, skirts and shoes for her.

"David told her she could come and live with him, and his friends - two girls. One of the girls, Hanka, later became David's wife. Gittel kept talking about Shulem and singing, *Vie Bistu*? (Where are you?)

"And that's how I know Gittel Rosen," said Alex. "The last thing I heard about her was that she and three other girls, who she knew from the camps, were living together in a guesthouse that the Polish Government had given them. He also heard that Gittel had been going around from town to town looking for me. "Where is she, Alex, do you have an address to give me?" I was most anxious to hurry this conversation along. "Don't worry," he said, "stay with me a few days and I'll show you around a bit." He looked at my face and smiled. I had to beg him for Gittel's address and then finally he gave it to me. She was near the town of Langenbila in the village of Sofiagura. He gave me a contact, a large bakery in Reichenbach run by some Jews. "These people are very nice," he said. "Tell them that you came from far away to look for a girl named Gittel from Sofiagura and they will help you."

Alex walked me to the front door. "Before you return home," he said, "stop at the DP camp in Frankfurt, Salzheim and see David Santzer and his wife Hanka."

David and Hanka were very happy to see me. "From Gittel's description I'd know you anywhere, Shulem," Hanka said. My visit with the Santzers was brief as I was very eager to meet up with Gittel, but I was also pleased that I met them both. Hanka recently died of emphysema.

Before continuing my search for Gittel, I decided to return home to Turkheim. I packed another overnight bag with leather, silk and two silver fox skins. I thought that I would need to do some trading in Poland; there I was no big shot!

I boarded the train: a cattle train with no seats. Memories came flooding back to me reminding me of the dark days of war. I thought about my mother and how she suffocated to death in a cattle train.

The train went to Czestochowa from where I took the bus to Reichenbach. It was quite a walk to the bakery, but I did not think too much about it. I was thinking of Gittel and how we'd both feel when we saw each other again. Suddenly, I was standing outside the bakery. I went in and told the baker that I was looking for Gittel Rosen who lived near Langenbila with three other girls. He said he knew her and that he would get someone with a horse and buggy to take me to Langenbila, and that he would come too. He wanted to tell Gittel that I was well, just to cushion the shock!

Then, all of a sudden, I saw the baker and Gittel approaching. I was hiding in an alleyway. She looked so beautiful, I knew that I was looking at someone that I loved very much. Little by little he brought her closer to me. Then she fell into my arms, crying. "SHULEM!!! I looked for you everywhere!" As I held her close to me, everything else seemed to disappear. It was wonderful. After all, we had known each other since childhood.

She told me everything that had happened to her and I told her everything that had happened to me.

The baker kindly paid for a room for us in a little hotel, in Reichenbach. "Get to know each other," he said, happy that we had found one another.

The next morning I told her that we should stay a while in Reichenbach. I had my overnight bag full of good stuff and the owner of the bakery told me to go to

Czestochowa to sell my goods for a top price. I needed to do some trading. Dressed smartly in a uniform jacket and an American blue hat I made my way to Czestochowa on the bus. I heard two Poles talking to each other; they were saying that a day before, the A.K. took fifteen Jews off that same bus, took them to the woods and shot them. Hearing this, I was glad I had my American uniform with me.

Soon after arriving, I met a man named Yidel that the baker in Reichenbach sent me to, and pretty soon we were bargaining. We spoke about this and that, and then I asked if he had connections to smuggle Gittel into Germany with me; I had an I.D. from the German government and she had nothing.

"Shush!" he said, and took me to one side. Under his breath he told me that were two brothers, Krulik, who knew how to get to the other side, to Germany. "Go look for them," he said.

I met up with the brothers and told them my story of how I was working for the American government. I had found my 'wife' and now we wanted to go back. The first brother did not say a word. He just stared at me, studying my face. Eventually, he looked over to the second brother and in a deep voice told me how much it would cost, and the route we would take, Poland to Leipzig; it was easier that way since the Russians were in charge.

I went back to Reichenbach and told Gittel about my meeting with the brothers. She agreed that this seemed the only way for her to go back with me. I kissed her hard, our future life together now a reality.

The Kruliks were well connected with German people and had hired a German with a small open truck. We traveled together with the brothers in the truck under cover of darkness, passing town after town, until finally we were in Leipzig. This was where we parted from the Kruliks. We shook hands and then we were on our way again, all the time traveling. It was several days later that we came to Germany and took the train to Munich, and from Munich to Turkheim.

The whole town knew that I had gone to bring Gittel back with me, and I think most of them came out to greet us. When Dora found out that I had gone to get Gittel, she moved out and left.

* * * * * *

Finding Gittel also resulted in finding out the bad news about my nephew Kuba. Kuba jumped off the train to Treblinka, and was hiding, when he met a farmer's daughter. They soon became a couple, and he pretended to be an Italian who came to look for his family. Kuba worked on the farm until the end of the war.

Miraculously Kuba and Gittel ran into each other in Lodz. They decided to meet again after a few days, and to go together to look for me. When Gittel arrived at the restaurant where they had arranged to meet, Kuba didn't show up. When Gittel told me the story, I asked the Military Governor to look into it, and he came back with the sad information: The murderers of the *Armia kriova* killed him. The farmer probably found out that he was Jewish, informed the A.K. and they murdered Kuba.

* * * * * *

Gittel was so happy when she saw my house. She loved everything about it: the living room, the piano, the flowers. She welcomed my friends to our home and they took to her straight away. Everyone loved her, especially me. Two weeks after I had brought Gittel to Turkheim we were married. Right from the start we decided that, just like my brother, we were going to live in America, and so sometime in 1946 we applied for a visa.

Up until the time of our emigration, I was determined that Gittel would not want for anything. I told the Berger Meister that we needed a maid and he sent us a German woman from a farm in the village. She cleaned and cooked for us and I paid her well.

Things were slowly returning to normal in Turkheim. Shops were starting to open and people seemed happier, but the hatred of Jews was still there even though it was not shown outwardly. No Jews participated in business in Turkheim. They did not open regular stores, they did whatever they could to make ends meet, even dealing on the black market. Most of their time though, they spent looking for relatives, sitting around trying to decide what to do and where to go. Israel or America?

I was working with *Aliyah Bet* at that time helping them send people to Israel. I was a Jabotinsky follower and knew many who would one day be great heroes of Israel. One of them, Menachem Begin, I knew from Warsaw. I remember him clearly.

Gittel and I were having a good life, but it seemed as though something was missing. One day I said to Gittel, "We have to start doing something!"

It was about this time that I received a phone call from Colonel Stern. "Hi Shulem, I'm calling from The States. Guess what, I've found your brother!" At first Colonel Stern could not find my brother but instead found a distant cousin of mine, also named Silberzweig, in Brooklyn. Stern told my cousin how he had met Shulem Silberzweig in Germany, and that Shulem was looking for his brother. My cousin told him that my brother had changed his name to Jack Silver and had a men's clothing business on 6th Avenue in New York. It was through this connection that Stern found my brother. I was so happy.

We started to write letters to each other and then packages began arriving from UNWRA, with rations. In his first letter to me, my brother asked who had survived from the family. It hurt me a lot to tell him that I was the only survivor.

I decided it was time to try to make some money. Until then I had worked with the CIC and the Military Governor; now I wanted to better myself. With the help of the American Military Governor, I received a special permit from a region in Germany called Algeier State (also called Shvaben). It called for all raw furs to be delivered and sold directly to me.

The Germans brought all different kinds of furs to me, including very rare ones, and I was very fair with my prices. There were a lot of butchers that had calves' skins, which by law had to be delivered to me. I stored the skins in a warehouse especially made to hold raw fur on the first floor of my house. Algeier had the nicest calves' skins which were a beautiful beige color, and were made up into beautiful coats. In a city called

Bakna, they bought the heavy calves' skins from me to make leather.

In Frankfurt, there was a big skin dealer, a Nazi named Shultz. Whenever I went to see him about buying skins, he would see me and shake in his boots. He knew that I had previously worked for the Americans. And yet he gave me whatever I wanted.

Also in Frankfurt, there was a big factory where they were dressing the skins. I took cigarettes and cognac, showed them my permit, and once a week organized a truck to load up raw skins: calf, rabbit, fox and stone-martin.

After a while, I noticed that one of the butchers did not deliver his skins to me. I came to his house one night and asked him where the skins were. "Don't play games with me, you know I can close your business!" I told him to come with me to the slaughterhouse. We went in and saw wet sacks. I told him to lift them; underneath there was a large pile of calf skins. I asked him to explain what they were doing there, and he said they were from a long time ago. I said, "don't tell me stories or you will know who Silberzweig is. Tomorrow morning, bring the skins to my house!" He did so, I paid him and told him, "Next time you do this you will be very sorry."

I made a deal with a German furrier in Kempten to buy my first fur machine; I could buy the machine if I agreed to give him a Persian lamb coat. I bought the coat from some Germans for chocolate.

I was building up my business, so I began looking for workers. There were many furriers and tailors who were *flechlinger* (refugees) from other countries: Hungary,

Czechoslovakia and Poland, and were looking for work. I employed these people to put lining in the coats, and to finish them.

The business was doing so well that I built a factory on the third floor of my home. People with fur stores from the surrounding towns of Mindelheim and Kempten soon found out about me, and they came to see me. They were interested in buying the fur coats. They came several times and each time brought gifts in addition to money. Word soon got around, and every Sunday people would line up to buy my coats. So many people came that I had four or five cars parked down-stairs at one time. I let them come up only one at a time. I was doing such enormous business and made so much money, that I didn't know what to do with it. All this was in 1947 and I was just thirty years old.

On March 8, 1947, our daughter, Rochelle (Shelley), was born. Her birth put our plans to emigrate on hold for a while, as we did not want to travel with a new baby. But that did not stop us from getting ourselves organized for when the time came to go.

The girlfriend of Alex Porzitcki, who was living near-by in Munich, was working with the American govern-ment at that time and recommended me to the American officers. They bought a lot of coats to send to their wives and girlfriends. I told them to send the money to my brother in New York; this way when I went to The States I would have some money there.

The coats I manufactured looked as though they were sable, but in fact they were made from Muskrat. Muskrat coats were as rare as diamonds after the war. All this time, I was still working hard trying to find rooms for survivors. I pushed the Germans out of their big houses and replaced them with survivors. One day, I received an anonymous hate letter. It said that if I did not stop doing this, they would kill me. I told the Governor about the letter. He said that it was impossible to tell who sent it and that I should be careful about what I was doing. I was not afraid, I had a gun and I made sure I took it everywhere with me.

I was feeling very good these days, but my heart still ached terribly. I never felt guilty that I had survived; everyone was fighting to survive and any feelings of guilt never entered my mind. Each one of us had to fight to survive, or die in the struggle. The Nazis made us feel that even their animals were more important than the Jews were. They made us feel less than animals. The fact that they gave us numbers instead of using our names was one way that they tried to dehumanize us. A number had no connection with a human being, like a name. A fly was more important than a Jew – a fly could fly away whenever it chose. We honestly did not believe that we would survive. We simply lived from one hour to the next, and one day to the next. And any stories about people killing each other, or selling each other out to survive, I simply do not believe.

Sol and Gloria

Gloria when Sol found
her, Poland

Graves, Turkheim

Sol with Maryek Ganz

Commemoration of Holocaust victims, Turkheim

With friends, Bad Reichenhall, Germany

Turkheim, 1945

Turkheim, 1947

Survivors gathering

Chapter 13
Preparations for America

On March 8, 1948 we invited over fifty people to our daughter's first birthday party. We had an orchestra, drinks, fish and geese; a special cook prepared everything. We all had a wonderful time, the party going on into the early hours of the morning.

Even though we were living in a nice house, and making lots of money, we had made up our minds to join my oldest brother Jack in America. We were waiting for the visa from two sources, the American government and from HIAS, the Hebrew Immigrant Aid Society; they helped people who wanted to immigrate to America.

Gittel and I decided to buy porcelain to take with us. A good friend of my brother Jack who lived in Hoff near Selp, also going to America, suggested I go to the Rosenthal factory in Selp. "If you're looking for the best, go there!" he said. "That's where I bought my things." I was so pleased that I took his advice. I bought some really nice, good quality porcelain figurines, a 120 piece porcelain dinner set with twenty-two karat gold all around, silver candelabras, specially made curtains, expensive tablecloths, paintings, and many other things for the house. After the war, they started to make things less expensive. Even so, it would take me a long time to put together everything we intended to take.

Gittel and I were starting to get anxious. We still had not received our visa to travel. About a week later, they called me in to the American Consulate in Munich. I had been to Munich many times before, traveling to Frankfurt through the Munich office to buy things. They started asking me questions about who I had in America and so on. Finally, they told me that I had from now, March, until June to organize and pack everything so we would be ready.

We had a lot of delicate things that needed special packing and handling. I hired the son of the Bürgermeister from Turkheim to help me, to ensure that things would not be broken on the way. I put him in charge of having special cases built for the trip. Someone told me to put a *tallis* and a *Siddur* on top of one case. "If the case is opened by a Jewish examiner, it'll help things along if he sees the *tallis*!"

I went home after my visa interview and waited until they let me know when my visa would be ready. In the meantime, I tried to sell all the furs I had. I made a mistake by telling the Germans I was going to America and they stopped buying from me. And then when my departure date was near, they wanted to pay pennies on the dollar. I practically gave away my two machines.

Because the Germans stopped buying from me, I found that I had a lot of silver foxes left. Every woman who went to America bought two silver foxes from me. I was the only one in Germany selling silver fox furs. The silver fox furs were very expensive. I bought them for around 100 marks and I sold them for about $100 a piece. I was a real moneymaker! I decided to take about eight foxes with me; I figured I would get a good price for them in America.

Four weeks before I left for America, I decided to

change some marks for dollars, so I went to the black market. I had Aliyete marks, which was a strong currency backed by the Americans, twenty-six marks to the dollar. A short time later, the mark went down to four to the dollar! I did not care that I lost a lot of money. My brother was waiting for me in America and that was all that mattered to me.

I received a phone call from the American Consulate letting me know that our visa had arrived and that they had paid for our passage. The person on the other end of the phone also mentioned the sailing date: two weeks later. There was so much to be done in so little time.

The keys of the house that the American Government had 'loaned' us, had to be returned to the mayor of Turkheim's office. The moment I learned of our sailing date, I arranged all the details for vacating the house. Later on I found that the Nazi Bergman moved back into the house when I left.

Suitcases and trunks were all over the place; there was hardly any room to move downstairs. We had twelve big trunks, each one the size of half a table. Hours before we were due to leave, I sold my car. I think the buyers purposely waited until the last minute knowing that I had no choice and would sell it at any price.

All our stuff packed and ready to go, we said goodbye to all the people that came to wish us luck. We left Turkheim in late June. By July 1949 all the Jews had left Turkheim, except for one who stayed because his wife was German.

As I was very friendly with the son of the Bürgermeister, he arranged for a big car and a truck to take us to the port of Bremen - a good six to eight hours' drive. When we arrived, we soon discovered that we would not be leaving right away; instead we were taken to some barracks. It was terrible. There, someone very official looking wrote our names and destination on our trunks, and took them to be loaded onto the ship, The General Hauzi - an army boat. We waited there for days until the ship was ready to go.

When we were finally allowed aboard the ship, Gittel, Shelley and I were taking our first step on our journey to make a new life for ourselves in America.

Everyone had a ticket with a cabin number on it. Gittel and Shelley had a cabin to themselves, but I was in a cabin down the hall from them. I was not too happy about that until I found out that I would be sharing a cabin with an old friend from Turkheim.

The first day at sea was terrible; a very bad storm tossed the boat up and down and from side to side. My daughter, Shelley, who was two years old at the time, almost fell off the ship into the sea. Thankfully, she was saved by one of the sailors. The boat tossing and turning was really horrible, I felt very seasick. Somehow the boat's movements did not seem to bother Gittel. She did not feel sick once.

The cabins were very comfortable with big bunks, but there was not enough air, so during the day we sat outside. For me, the smell of the fish outside was too much and turned my stomach. To this day, I have never gone on another boat trip!

One night as we lay in our cabins listening to the sound of the propellers, and hearing the dolphins following the boat from behind, a woman suddenly shouted out, "Lights, I see lights! We must be arriving in New York!"

The lights were beautiful, what a sight to see. Everyone was shouting and screaming, we were all smiling and happy. It was very exciting. Everyone began pushing one another to get a better view of the lights and the Statue of Liberty from the rails at the sides of the boat. There were maybe 400-500 people on the boat; it was very crowded. We arrived at the Pier at 49th Street, on the West Side of Manhattan. The trip had taken eight days.

Turkheim, 1947

*On the ship
to New York,
Sol, Shelly and
Gloria*

Chapter 14
Arrival, and Starting Another New Life

We watched as everyone's luggage was unloaded from the boat. At first, we could not find our twelve trunks, until suddenly Gittel shouted out, "There! There they are on the pier!" By the time we reached our stuff, customs agents had already started examining people's luggage right there on the pier. I stood beside my things and waited for my turn. I was sweating heavily, it was July 3rd and it was very hot outside.

One of the customs agents was already coming to process our cases. As he came towards me, I could see on his face that he was Jewish and the name on his nametag proved it. He opened my case and on top he found my *tallis*. I did not say a word to him, but for a brief second he looked at me, and then he stamped the luggage and said, "OK, proceed." In 1949 it still pretty easy to get into America.

At the port, they were looking for old and new items that people might be transporting into the country. Items such as the porcelain and silver I was carrying. It was considered 'smuggling', and we had to pay port taxes on everything. This is a good start in a new country, I thought.

We proceeded to leave the pier when I heard someone yelling, "Shulem, Shulem, Shulem!" I turned around. It was my brother, standing beside several people from my extended family, who were also there to meet us. Jack was waving his hand at me, my brother whom I had seen only once before when he came from Germany to my sister's wedding in the early 1930's; he had left home before I was born.

Standing beside my brother Jack was his second wife, (his first was killed in Germany), my two cousins, Daniel's sons, and their wives, as well as my cousin Molly, Yisrael's daughter. The greeting they gave us was so warm, it did not seem as though we did not really know any of these people. They took us to their hearts. "Wait, wait!" I said, before we took another step. I had a Leica camera with me, for my brother.

There was tight security on the pier and Jack reassured me that it was a good idea to leave our luggage there for the time being. "OK," I said, happy not to have to *shlep* it around with us.

From the pier we all went on to Jack's place. Jack and his family were living in Manhattan, at the corner of 44th Street and 9th Avenue. I can still remember the building, it was a nice old building. He also had a summer place in Rockaway, Edgemere. In those days, it was like the Hamptons are today. People rented bungalows for the summer there. The area where they were living in Manhattan was called *Little Hollywood* as many movies were being filmed across the street. We stayed for a day or two at Jack's home and then he had a surprise up his sleeve for us; he took us to his rented bungalow in Rockaway near the beach. It was large enough for the whole family. It was so wonderful and relaxing. I couldn't remember the last time I felt so relaxed.

One evening, as we were all sitting on the beach toasting marshmallows on a small fire, Jack suggested we go for a stroll along the shore. "I can't believe you're here," he said. I could not believe it myself. Then Jack asked me how it was that I survived and not Monyek, Leibel, Zelda, nor Salla. I told him that I had been in seven camps, and that I just lived day to day. It was not my choice that made me survive. Many of the people who survived were the Kapos or others who had worked with the SS. Not me.

I was a pure clean person; everybody who was with me in the camps knew that too. I never knowingly did anything to harm another Jew. There were many people who did dirty things in the camps, and when the war ended they were beaten up. But on the whole, most of the people in the camps were like me. Very few were made of the stuff to be Kapos. The Kapos came from a background that was very bad to begin with. The Kapos always tried to save their skins.

I had been relaxing on the beach and enjoying the good life for some time. One morning Jack took me to see his store. It was on 6th Avenue between 45th and 46th Streets and occupied both the first and second floors. Jack showed me around, proud of his achievement. There were suits, tuxedos, haberdashery and much more.

I looked around the store to see if there was anything I could do to be of help. I fixed the shelves, straightened out the merchandise, but my heart was not in the *shmatte* (clothing) business. My heart was set on the fur business.

Jack and I stayed in the city during the week; on weekends I went to Rockaway and spent time with Gittel – now called Gloria – and Shelley. My brother tried hard to act and feel as though he was my brother.

For me it was not the same, since I knew him only through photographs. I would not say that it was strange between us, because we both made an effort to be like brothers; he was the reason I came to America. Whatever our differences, it was still nice to know that I had a brother. All my friends went to Israel; if it were not for Jack, I would have gone there too.

When the summer was over, Jack went back to his place in Manhattan, and the rest of the family to their homes. Gloria, Shelley and I stayed in the house until the end of summer. Jack and his family had been so kind and supportive, but at the back of my mind I had felt uneasy not knowing what would become of us. The summer spent at the beach was very nice, but I was still anxious about finding a job and starting my new life in America.

My uncle Daniel was living on Pelham Parkway in the Bronx. He had left word with his sons that when I came to America, and if he was no longer living, that we could take over his apartment. As it happened, he died shortly before we arrived.

At that time it was very difficult to get an apartment in New York because of all the Army veterans who came back after the war and needed a place to live. I was lucky to get my uncle's apartment.

A cousin of mine, Sam Silver, who had been sharing the apartment with my uncle, organized a little van to take us to the apartment, which was located on Cruger Avenue. It was a small apartment and not in particularly good condition. There was a little foyer, kitchen, one bedroom, and an area that I suppose was considered the dining area, as there was a dining table there by the window.

When Gloria stepped into the apartment, from looking at her face I could tell that she was not happy with her surroundings. Shelley ran around quite content, but Gloria was very depressed. "We had a lovely house in Turkheim," she said, "what have we come to?" I took her hand and said to her, "You looked around this place and saw something that didn't make you happy. I promise you that in one week, maybe two, I'll have it looking like a palace for my two little princesses." Apartments those days were scarce, I did not tell Gloria that we were lucky to have it. Jack recommended someone that we could hire to come and fix up the apartment. I washed the walls myself. After just one week it was already starting to take shape. In two weeks, the smile was returning to Gloria's face. "You see," I told her, "a palace!" I started to bring the cases that I had put in storage and unpacked all our personal items. Some things we left in the bags and put in the corner.

It was while I was having lunch one day with Jack that I asked him about the fur business, and where it was. This question had been on my mind for quite some time. Jack had been so kind to me, teaching me about the shmatte business, I felt bad asking him. He did not think anything of the question and told me right off. "The fur business in this country is no good. If you think you can make money like you did over there, forget it!" And he slapped me on my back and went back to work. Later, I asked someone else about it and I was told that the fur trade could be found on 7th Avenue from 26th to 30th Streets.

In Poland we were in the import and export business.

We had a lot of experience doing business with America, where we sent them raw skins and also imported skins that were in demand in Poland. I remember as a child hearing about the Steiner Brothers. One of the brothers, Leon Steiner lived in Warsaw and was in the fur business. He was the middleman that we dealt with. Two other brothers, George and Meyer Steiner, lived in America, each with their own fur business.

Meyer owned a whole building at 214 West 30th Street. He was a skin dealer. The next morning I did not go to the store with Jack as I usually did, instead I went to the market to see the Steiner brothers. When I went in, straight away I was asked my name. "Shulem Silberzweig," I replied, "Oh, Silberzweig." This was George Steiner, he seemed interested in me. "Are you Yossel's son?" he asked. I told them I was his youngest. He immediately called his brother over and introduced me. They started to ask me a lot of questions about what happened to my family, especially Monyek; he was well-known in the fur business. They were very sad when I told them that everyone, except Jack who was here in America, was murdered.

I asked the brothers if it was possible for them to find me a job in the fur business. "You want a job?" Meyer said. Then they looked at each other and smiled. "You don't need a job. We'll put you in business!" And then they became serious. "That is, if you do what we tell you to do. You look like a very capable young man!" Then, they asked me if I wanted a cigar. I said "no thank you". They both smoked big cigars. They asked if I would like a cup of coffee. I said no to that as well.

"OK," said Meyer. "So come and sit down and tell us what you've been doing, and then we'll tell you a little bit about the business we run."

This was in 1949 and I was thirty-two years old, still wet behind the ears according to some people, but what I had gone through, most people would never experience in their whole lives.

They listened while I told them what I did in Germany. When I finished, George pulled out a handkerchief and blew his nose. "OK! That was then and now is now," he said.

Meyer lit a big cigar and settled himself down in a huge leather chair behind his desk. "We're very big dealers in Persian lamb, and import from Russia and South Africa," he started to tell me. The brothers went on to say that they would put together bundles of skins for me to take on the road to sell to furriers. Meyer smiled. "The customers will be very happy to see you," he said. George nodded, agreeing.

I phoned Jack and told him that I had to see him about something. I think he had a good idea about what I was going to say. He knew that the *shmatte* business was not for me and I was not for it.

I had already prepared what I was going to say to Jack and he took it very well. "It's nothing personal, but I just can't see myself in the *shmatte* trade," I told him. "The fur business is what I know best." Jack put a hand on my shoulder. "You have to do what you think is right for you," he said. "Nothing will ever change the fact that we're brothers, so do what you want and I wish you all the best. No hard feelings!"

I had found my brother and nothing was ever going

to come between us. "We'll see each other on weekends, right?" he said. Jack was concerned about how I would get around. He warned me that this was America and I had to be careful.

Meanwhile, I found out about a guy named Paul Stein originally from Mesrich, who was now in Cleveland and would be willing to work with me. The person who gave me this information was someone I had met on the street, a man named Aaron Crook. I met Crook on Seventh Avenue " He said, "Oh, you are Shulem Silberzweig!" Crook used to bring raw furs to us in Warsaw from Chelm. Crook was known as a conniver but I decided to trust him anyway. Aaron Crook said that in 1946, Paul arrived as a refugee in America settling in Brooklyn where he opened a store (I later learned that Paul had been a policeman in the Mesrich Ghetto).

Paul's family had been collecting raw skins from trappers all over Poland. Mesrich was known as a center for raw skins. Paul's father's company paid the highest price for them. They also bought the hair from pigs and sold it all over the world. The raw bristles, the hair from pigs, were used for brushes. I asked Aaron for Paul's telephone number and he gave it to me.

I made contact with Paul, introducing myself as Shulem Silberzweig, the youngest son of Yossel Silberzweig. Paul asked about my family and he especially wanted to know about Monyek and Leibel. He was sad when I told him that they had both been murdered in the camps.

"Do you remember that your father did business with us?" he said. "In Warsaw, my father brought you raw furs and your father bought them." The world had changed since those days.

I had some Persian skins in bundles for coats that I got from the Steiner brothers. Paul said that he would go to the furriers with me and help me sell them. I felt excited at the idea of getting back into the fur business. But first I had to get to Cleveland. Where was that?

Jack helped me get to the train. He was worried that I did not know where I was going or how to get there. "Don't worry," I told him, trying to appear confident. "After all, didn't I travel all over Germany by myself and manage quite well?"

While I was working for my brother I tried to learn English at the same time. I attended night school several times a week and after a while I was speaking like a native. Well almost!

We loaded everything onto the train. The boxes of furs were put under my seat for safekeeping. I tied a string from the boxes to my hand, so if anyone tried to move the boxes I would feel it.

The trip lasted all night and we arrived in Cleveland about 7 AM. Paul Stein was already waiting for me on the platform as the train pulled into the station "Hello" he greeted me with a hug, "I've brought my car," he said, and pointed to an old jalopy. The Kaiser must have been quite nice in its day, but now it looked as though it did not have another mile left in it. "I know what you're thinking," he said, helping me to load up the bags of furs, "but when I have the money for gas it gets me around town."

Paul lived above a store, with his wife and two sons, on 123rd Street on the East Side of Cleveland, the worst part of town. Compared to him, I was living like a king in New York. His business was not very successful, and he was just able to make ends meet. We had arranged that everything I sold, he would get a 5% commission. At one store they bought one of the bundles. The next customer we did a little better, they bought two bundles. Every store we went to they bought something from us. We did very well that first day.

The second day we traveled more and sold more. We sold almost 75% of the stock. I was hoping that Paul would not ask me where I got the merchandise from, because I did not want him going behind my back to do business on his own. Not too far from the house was a telephone and I made a collect call to the Steiner brothers. I told them how well I was doing, and that I was thinking about returning to New York the following week to take more merchandise and head out again. They were very happy that I had done so well.

For a couple of weeks I went back and forth, leaving some of the bundles with Paul to sell and then returning with fresh goods. All this traveling around and yet I always managed to find the time to see Gloria and Shelley. Gloria could not believe what I had accomplished.

One day, I called up Aaron Crook, just to say hello. "Sol," he said, "I've something very important to tell you. You'll make a lot of money. Meet me in the market." Aaron knew somebody in the Muskrat business with Rayback Levine, furriers. Apparently, they were stuck with 500 coats they could not sell and would probably be going bankrupt. Excitedly, Aaron filled me in:

"These days a coat like this would cost between $180 to $200 a piece, wholesale. If you've got cash, you can buy 100 coats for $100 a piece. Then you can sell them at a nice profit."

I went down to Rayback Levine to see the coats. They were in good condition and so I asked how much they were selling them for. If the price was fair I said I would buy fifty, provided I could pick out my own coats. They agreed and a deal was struck. I contacted Paul and told him that I would be bringing down some Muskrat coats at very reasonable prices. I told Aaron Crook that he would make a commission from the seller if I bought.

Five thousand dollars was a lot of money to withdraw from the bank, and Gloria was worried. But I was certain that I could sell the coats. I had a brilliant idea. I marked every coat on the leather inside the coats with my name so Rayback Levine could not change them around. I then packed everything up in boxes, and paid to have them delivered to Meyer Steiner. I told Steiner that somebody had given me the coats to sell. I did not tell him that I bought them.

I also took Persian bundles to Cleveland with the coats. Paul was waiting at the station and was surprised to see how many boxes I had. We loaded up his car and headed for his place. I told Paul that whenever we leave the goods in his house, someone must be home. He assured me that his wife would be home. At this time, Muskrat coats were very big deal.

Paul and I went from store to store selling the coats. By the end of the first week we had sold twenty coats; we were doing very well. I made good money and Paul earned a nice commission. I suddenly remembered Jack trying to discourage me from going into the fur business. Now, just a few months after my arrival in the United States he saw that I was OK.

It was not long after this, that Paul came and asked me to make him a partner. "I'll do the hustling," he said. "You take it easy, relax in New York. You can trust me, I'll bring in more business." I told him that I would think it over. I went back to New York and tried to contact the Muskrat people, but found out that the only stock that remained was damaged. It was then I remembered that Paul told me how he used to buy wild mink from the trappers and other minks from the farmers. I decided to do the same and we went together to the farmers and trappers.

Chapter 15
Royal Mink is Born

It was 1950, business was good and the money was rolling in so I bought myself a car, a black 1947 Pontiac. I drove everywhere in that car, to Cleveland overnight with merchandise and back again, to the farmers to buy the raw minks, to the trappers to buy raw wild mink. At this point wild mink was more expensive than the farmed. We also bought some top rate red foxes and warehoused them.

One time I decided that I did not want to run my car into the ground and suggested we drive Paul's Kaiser for a change. We had arranged with some trappers to view their merchandise, and we were driving towards the Great Lakes area. From out of nowhere a snowstorm started. The temperature began dropping rapidly. It was getting colder and colder by the minute. "What's the matter with you, put the heater on," I begged Paul and wrapped my coat tightly around me. It was so very, very cold.

Paul looked over to me and smiled. "What heater? There isn't any!" The windshield was beginning to freeze up. Paul jumped out of the car and began rubbing salt on it. I had had enough at this time. "I don't want to drive like this," I told him. "Let's stop at the next hotel. Don't worry, it's on me!" It seemed we were not too far from a hotel. Paul parked his jalopy and we went in.

The lobby was full of people. I went up to the desk

and I spoke to the clerk there. He had a German accent and I started to talk in German. I knew straight off that he was not a Jew, but I did not think he knew that I was. "You need a room?" he asked politely. I told him that I did. "No problem," he said. "You'll get a nice room, don't worry."

The area that Paul and I stopped in was right in the heart of mink farming country. The next day I went over to the clerk, we already knew each other by name, and I said, "I'll give you a $100 if you call all the farmers around here and tell them to bring some minks here by sled. Tell the farmers that a buyer came from Europe." I always came up with ideas.

Usually the farmers would send their furs to The Hudson Bay Auction Company. This was an old company that used to buy raw furs from the Indians and Eskimos and pay them with food. Now the company financed the farmers to raise the minks and not to sell to local buyers, only to The Hudson Bay Auction Company. I knew that the farmers used to leave the best quality furs on the side for themselves. My idea was to buy the best quality. The clerk made good on his word. He called all the farmers in the area and told them I had come from Germany and I would pay them top dollars in cash. I told the clerk that we needed a room with a table and fluorescent light. He arranged for us to use the banquet hall! I couldn't believe it.

The first farmer brought in several big boxes filled with mink. Straight away we started to look over the merchandise and rate them. Paul Stein had a good eye. He was born to know raw skins: the hair inside, the leather outside. We bought thousands of dollars worth of minks at that hotel. It was just before Christmas and the farmers needed money for the holidays. They were happy and so were we! When the snow started to melt we wrapped up business, began packing up our goods and headed back to the warehouse in Cleveland.

Once back in Cleveland we had to find a customer. What we found was the biggest and most famous furrier in Cleveland: Sikra Furs. The owner was a Czech German from Sudeten. I went up to him and introduced myself. We started to talk in German, since my German was better than my English. I told him I had some nice minks to sell, silver blue mink, which was a very big deal in those days. It was a new color that had just been introduced. He liked what he saw, and he liked the price. He gave me a check for $15,000. This was three times more than the price that I paid for them, and I still had a lot of minks left over. Later I found out that for him it was a bargain.

The bank was closed so I had to wait until the following morning to cash the check. At the counter I asked the teller if I could cash the check. He excused himself, and went into another room and called Sikra to make sure that the check was genuine. On another occasion, I tried to bring Sikra some more merchandise from the farmers and he refused. Later I found out that it was because I cashed his check right away!

I decided it was time to start up a company with Paul. Previously we were not a regular company we just took furs and sold them, but now we were going to make it official. We registered a company by the name of the Great Lakes Fur Company.

I remembered some people that I had met in

Cleveland had a big fur cleaning plant at 200 West 14th Street. I went and spoke to them about renting space. They said, "Sure!" And we shook hands on it. That same day I contacted Schaffer Furs in New York and bought some merchandise from them: Stonemartin and mink scarves. They were excellent items, so I had them shipped to Cleveland. I also brought some other merchandise from New York.

Paul and I put up an iron grid and hung up the goods. We were in business!

One day Paul called me. Someone had cut open the gate and taken some of the scarves that were hanging in our warehouse. People over there said that someone from the inside did it. It was later that I found out Paul himself had done it. I don't know exactly how he did it but I decided to forget it, never mentioning to him that I knew.

The Great Lakes Fur Company, with Paul as my partner, was going well, perhaps too well. It seemed that behind my back things were cooking between Leon Steiner and Paul. Steiner knew Paul's father before the War. Steiner had spoken to Paul, not to me, about taking him on as a partner too. It was all arranged between them that Steiner would do the buying for him at cheap prices. When word reached me I said, "No, who needs a third partner!" That's when Paul laid his ultimatum on me. "Either take Steiner for a third partner or I'll leave!"

We did not need three partners but in the end, I decided to take Steiner on for a little while. I knew him well from the old country, and his brothers had helped me a lot. All the time that we had a three-way partnership I felt that Paul and Leon Steiner wanted to push me out. Before they had a chance, I left. That was in 1954.

I was spending most of my days and nights working in Cleveland. I did not have much time to spend with my family, perhaps the occasional weekend. I was missing Shelley growing up; she was already seven years old. Working hard made me forget the past. I was thinking less and less about the war and concerning myself with the future, and being successful.

I started another business with a Greek named Mike Strudges. This guy used to be my subcontractor. His idea was that whenever I went away on business he would take care of things on the home front. His idea sounded good and I felt that I could trust him, so I went into partnership with him. Mike wanted to put in money rather than merchandise, promising that he would bring in $150,000 worth of business a year. I put in merchandise and said that I would bring in a quarter of a million.

We called our company *Royal Mink* after an idea that came to me as I drove to work one day. I spotted a sign for *Royal Tires* and thought it the perfect name. I spent a lot of time traveling cross-country buying and selling minks: New York, Pennsylvania, Ohio, Illinois, Michigan, Wisconsin, Massachusetts. All this traveling, sometimes weeks at a time, I missed my family a lot. I was out there making money; $20,000, $30,000, $50,000, $80,000 a shot selling furs and Mike was staying behind pretending to work.

Mike's promise to bring in $150,000 a year in business never materialized. He made just $30,000. I didn't say anything. When Rosh Hashana and Yom Kippur came around I told him that I would take the time off. "The Jews have too many holidays," he said. That sounded anti-Semitic to me. When he said that, I wanted to hit him. "How much business did you bring in all year?" I asked. "$30,000," was his reply, to which I responded: "I already got over $100,000 and the best time is still ahead."

Once I came back unexpectedly to find him lying on the couch playing the stock market, not taking care of the business. After almost two years as business partners I saw that he was not living up to his part of the bargain. Also, I found that he had been doing things behind my back. One of these things was making contact with other people, other Greeks, to form a partnership. I told him that I wanted out. He was not too upset. He went into business with some big shots, The Mangakis Brothers. We started the partnership in 1954. By 1956 we split up.

During the time Mike and I were partners, my son Morris and daughter Rivka were born. Rivka was named after Gloria's mother, Rivka Leah, and Morris was named after my father and my wife's father – Moishe Yossel, Morris Joe. We were living on Pelham Parkway at this time.

In Pelham Parkway there lived a Jewish guy named Jack. He was a quiet guy and seemed honest, working for a furrier named Abrams, who was buying raw skins from us. At this time, I was working on my own but it was a strain on me. The traveling and leaving the stock of valuable furs with strangers was very hard. Jack was a good furrier; he had learned a lot while working for Abrams. I told him that I wanted to go into partnership with someone and I thought he would be ideal. Jack told me that he could not promise me any business since he did not have any from before. But he put up some money, and so did I, and so we became partners.

I hustled to build the business and slowly we built it up into something really good. We made a very fine product inside and outside and we were at the top of the fur trade. The partnership was going fine and we were making lots of money. I would take the cash customers paid for our goods and put it in the safe; checks I put in the drawer. I did not think to check that everything was in its place, I trusted Jack. I put my faith in him even though I did not know him very well.

One day in October, I was on the road and I was feeling very cold, I was wearing a thin raincoat. I asked Jack to go to my wife, one block away and to pick up my warmer coat and to send it along with the next shipment. Quite calmly he said, "Tell your wife to bring it to me!" I almost fell flat on my face. That was when I knew that something was wrong. I had a bad feeling about this.

I went home immediately. A funny feeling told me to go and check the safe. I knew that there was supposed to be about $30-40,000 dollars in it. I opened the safe and I saw no money. "JACK!" I yelled. "Where's the money?" When he heard me yell out to him, Jack ran upstairs to a private retailer who we used to do business with, who was the comedian Jerry Lewis's uncle. Jack was afraid. He told the guy upstairs everything. Later, I learned that Jack had loaned my money to his brother-in-law to go into business.

I was working so hard hustling day and night, leaving my wife and small children alone and he did this to me. It was unbelievable that he could open the safe without my permission and just help himself to the money. To me, this was the act of a thief. I made up my mind there and then that I did not want to stay with him anymore. The trust I had for him was lost.

We split the merchandise, and for the money he took, I took back in merchandise. I learnt a lot that day. One of the lessons I learnt was not to put my trust too easily in people.

It was 1956. I still had a business to run. I kept all the customers from when Jack and I were partners. I knew where to go and who to sell to. Whenever I came to a town I found out who was honest and who was not, who were the people I could trust. I was finished dealing with thieves!

I decided that partners were not for me and I would run the business myself. Gloria found someone to take care of the children and she came to watch the show-room. Everyone liked Gloria, she knew how to answer people's questions and if she wanted to know something when I was away, she would just call me on the phone. The whole crew who were working for me knew what to do while I was out of town.

In 1958 I traveled to Norway, Denmark and Sweden to buy raw goods. At this time, colored mink such as blue, and light gray, called "blue shadow" and "gray shadow" mink was very much in demand, and they were raising these animals for these colors in Scandinavia. By now, everyone knew the fine quality of my coats and knew the name *Royal Mink*. I did not need any partners. I was a big success on my own. I was known as "the ref", short for refugee.

The landlord of the building, Sidney Bernstein, owned ten buildings in the fur market, and his brother-in-law was an agent for my building. The brother-in-law had seen my fur coats, they were as good as Bergdorf Goodman's or Tiffany's, and he ordered the same to be made for his wife and daughter. We made him two gorgeous coats. At the time I wanted to move to 150 West 30th Street; big buyers were in this building. You had to pay $50,000 just for the key to a loft. It was the best building in the market. One day Sidney Bernstein called me and told me to come and see him.

He said that I could have a place on 150 West 30th Street, and pay only the rent money. The place was dirty but we cleaned it up and moved in. That was in 1960 and we are still there today. When we moved in, on February 1, 1960, we made a very big party and invited all our best customers. There were over 200 people, mostly from the fur trade. I received gifts: someone gave me a Remington typewriter, someone else gave me a vacuum cleaner; I felt like I had finally arrived. After only eleven years in America, I was so happy at how much I had achieved.

Sol with model

Chapter 16
Confronting the Labor Union

As soon as I started to be successful, the Union started making trouble for me. The new building was unionized and the Union was very strong. The furriers were part of the meat cutters' union. The union leaders were more like gangsters. The business agent of the Union was a terrible person named Maginski, and heading the Union was someone named George Stafsky. In those days all work had to go through the Union. If you contracted out work, and the Union found out, they would come down on you like a ton of bricks. Sometimes even your workers were known to report you, the Union was so strong.

Gloria had excellent taste in clothes. When the guys from the Union saw her they thought I was a big shot, so it was important for me not to give out contracting. I heard more than once of people getting beaten up by the Union.

This particular time I contracted out, the garment workers came and sewed but they did not nail. Nailing was supposed to be done at my place. One of my workers named Charlie told the Union that they saw garments nailed, that they did not make, and so they must have come from outside. The Union quickly came and asked questioned about these garments. In no time I was facing an impartial chairman, a middleman between the Union and a business, and was put on trial. The chairman was not really impartial. He was 99%

biased toward the union. I was accused of contracting out, and going against the rules. The punishment was a $5,000 fine. The only way I could get my workers back to work was if I agreed to pay the fine of $5,000. Everyone hired contractors, it was standard practice.

Two of my workers were really bad guys: Charlie who was Greek, and a Jewish man, made my life a misery but I couldn't fire them because of the Union. A month later, once again they found garments that were contracted. This went on for several years until I thought I would break.

There was a dealer in the market, a Jewish guy from Warsaw, named Charlie Reich who was closely connected to the Union and Stafsky. We made an agreement that every year I would give $5,000 to Stafsky and I would be left alone for a year. I figured I was safe, but I was not.

It seemed that some very big companies in the building were jealous of me and they were speaking to the Union against me. I was threatened with strikes, and more strikes. I went to the impartial chairman and paid $10,000 fines, not just once but twice. By now I was reaching the end of my rope, but could do nothing about it. Once, I wanted to see what I could do about all this but it reached the situation that a henchman from the Union pushed me away and didn't let me into my own place of business. The Union was too strong for me.

I found out that the henchman's name was R.Gold, and that his daughter rented a bungalow in the same arca as my summer home. It happened that someone introduced me to her. She seemed pleasant enough and so I said to her, "Please talk to your father, I have a wife and three children. I was in concentration camps..." I pleaded with her to speak to him. She said she would.

On Monday morning I went back to the building and again he refused to let me in. The following weekend I went back up to my summer home and saw his daughter. "I thought you were going to speak to your father," I said. She told me that her father was angry with her for getting mixed up in his business.

Everyone had trouble, but I had more than most; R. Gold and the others in the Union saw to that. When I was away, they used to call up late at night and call my wife dirty names. Later I changed my home phone number to an unlisted one.

Previously, FBI agents came to me and asked me if Charlie Reich was connected with the Union. I said I didn't know. This time when Gold didn't let me in, I decided that the Union went too far and I had enough. I decided that it was time that the FBI knew what was going on with the Union. I called the telephone number they had given me the first time. FBI agents asked me what the problem was and I told them everything I knew: the obscene telephone calls, how the Union had taken $172,000 from me between all the payoff money and fines during all the years, and when I had no more money to give them how I gave them my compensation for slave labor money I received from Germany. One thing I did not tell them though about Charlie Reich and the protection money. When I left to go home I was happy about one thing; Washington was starting to go after the Union. They asked me to come and see them in Washington.

While I was in Washington I saw two officers. One of them spotted the number on my arm and asked me which camp I was in. I told them the last camp I was in was Dachau. They asked what year that was. I said 1945 when they took us on the death march. He said he could not believe it. "I was one of the soldiers in the 1st Army who freed Dachau", he said. The two officers started to feel sorry for me and they gave me a hotline number to call if I had any more trouble. I was pleased that these FBI officers were on my side. The local police precinct in New York was in with the Union and they were unresponsive.

When the Union found out that I had gone to Washington, they stood outside my place to stop the merchants from getting things to me. The Union beat up people who they saw carrying my merchandise. One contractor who was beaten with a baseball bat later died in the hospital. To avoid the Union, I had boxes delivered to Charlie Reich. I packed them at his place and made them ready for shipping. He was already afraid of what I might tell the FBI about him.

The FBI tried to call Stafsky at the Union, and he ignored them a few times. Then the FBI came to me and asked me if I could show them who Stafsky and R. Gold were. "No problem!" I told them. "I'll sit with you in your car tomorrow morning across the street from the Union and point them out to you." Every morning Stafsky and Gold who were both very tall, walked to the fur market and looked around to see who was carrying boxes with merchandise, and then walked back to the Union offices on 26th Street between 7th and 8th Avenue. (The union is no longer there. FIT, Fashion Institute of

Technology has taken its place.) The following morning R. Gold and Stafsky came to the market. There was no mistaking Stafsky, he was a giant of a man around seven feet tall and always wore a leather coat, just like the Gestapo.

"That's R. Gold and the tall one's Stafsky." I pointed out to the FBI agent sitting in the car. The FBI agents got out of the car, walked right up to them, flashed their badges and said, "FBI you're under arrest!" They grabbed hold of R.Gold and Stafsky and handcuffed them. Stafsky did not say a word, he did not believe that this was happening to him He always thought that he was like *The Godfather*, above the law.

The whole market knew that I was the guy who called in the FBI, and that any time they were called they would come immediately. One time, the Union stopped me from going to Charlie Reich's store. Straight away, I called the hotline. Almost immediately two police cars, and three motorcycles with sirens blaring, arrived. The Union guys did not hang around. They ran away. The next morning, I found out that a Greek named Simon Atlas, hired by the Union as a guard, was so afraid when he saw the police he dropped dead of a heart attack.

One day the FBI Agents told me that there was going to be a trial against the Union. Many people warned me that the Union would kill me. "They'll put you in cement shoes in the East River!" I said, "I'm not worried. Hitler didn't kill me and neither will they!"

I decided that I had better hire a good lawyer. I was recommended to a Mr. Schindler. When we arrived at court, they were all sitting there: Stafsky, Maginski,

Charlie Huff, Vice President of the Union under Stafsky, R. Gold. They were all sitting there.

I was called to the witness stand. "Point out Stafsky, R. Gold, Maginski and Charley Huff!" I pointed straight at them. "What did R. Gold do to you?" I told them. "How did the Union people threaten you?" I told them everything from 1957 until that day of the trial. The Union cost me $172,000.

When the trial was over, we went outside through the back entrance. Stafsky spent three years in jail, Charlie Huff two years, R. Gold three years – in fact he died in jail. The old union was disbanded, and I was the guy who did it to them! After this the Greeks took over the new union and things changed. I walked one day to 345 Seventh Avenue. Years later, after he was released from jail, Stafsky saw me in the elevator and was afraid to get in. The same Stafsky who once told me to go back to Germany! And he was the strongest man of the Union - the worst gangster! Since then, I have been able to do my business as a free American citizen without being afraid.

Chapter 17
Business in Europe

In the 1960's, business became difficult in the United States. Some of my customers from Switzerland asked me, "Why don't you come to Switzerland, you can do big business here." I thought about it and decided to try to make a collection. Gloria and I put together some sixty units and shipped them to Zurich.

I booked myself into a nice hotel, the Carleton Elite, on the Banhoff Strasse, which was in the business district, and waited for the goods to arrive. I did not have long to wait. The shipping company I was working with called *Natural*, cleared the goods for me and delivered them to my hotel. The very next day I put on a special show in the showroom at the hotel. First I called on my customer, Peltz Paradis, who was very famous in Switzerland. The owner came out with her buyers to look over the collection. I was very anxious while they picked out some merchandise. I managed to sell eight or nine pieces, which was very good.

I had a model, who had worked with other furriers and was now working for me; she knew many people and had a lot of connections. I told her I would take care of her if she connected me with other buyers in Switzerland. She said that she would, and kept to her word. She contacted a lot of people who had stores in Zurich and Basel and told them they should come in to see my line. She even scheduled appointments with these people. The furriers in Switzerland were very anxious to buy American merchandise at this time. They heard that someone from *Royal Mink* in America was in town to show their line, and they made appointments. At that time, *Royal Mink* was the trade name I used to sell in Europe and *Luxurious Furs* to sell in the United States. Both companies belonged to me, *Sol Silberzweig, Inc.*

Early the following morning we were ready to show the line. I was impressed as to how quickly the people made up their minds what to buy. We did quite well. I sold merchandise to some people who came from Basel and was pleased that they paid straight away. In the States you had to wait months for the money and then sometimes you were lucky if you were paid in the end; sometimes the customers went bankrupt and you were not paid at all.

The model came up with a good suggestion. "Rent a car, and take the merchandise to Lausanne. And we could also go to Bern, and Basel, maybe even Geneva!" I still had thirty-five pieces left to sell and I had nothing to lose.

We started early in the morning, our first stop Bern and after that Basel. At both places we sold a few pieces. The model thought she would help me out with the language as she spoke French, English and German. But it was easy for me to communicate since I was also able to speak Swiss Deutsch, which was very similar to German. From Basel we went on to Lausanne. I was very impressed by the beautiful stores there.

We booked into the *Hôtel de la Paire*: the model in her room, and me and my furs in another. The furs did not leave my sight! At breakfast the next morning I met a Frenchman who said he was a furrier. He spoke no English or German, only French, so I was grateful for my model's help, as she was fluent in the language. The guy told me that he owned a store in the old town of Lausanne. I mentioned the name *Royal Mink* and straight away he bought two light coats from me.

I decided it was time to go home; I needed to check on my factory and merchandise. But before we left I figured we could try one or two more customers, after all people from all over the world came to Lausanne to shop. There was a store called *Canto*. I introduced myself and the owner asked what I had to show him. The only merchandise I had was what I had left in my room. So I said, "Come up to my hotel room and I'll show you!"

The owner came up to my room, saw what I had, liked what he saw, and bought several pieces. It was then I knew that I was on to a good thing in Lausanne. There were six furriers on one street. I could do very well there.

I went back to the USA and put together a nice collection of a hundred pieces. We packed them in big heavy boxes and shipped them off. When I arrived back at the hotel in Zurich the model was waiting for me, and together we went to the airport to clear the furs with customs. An official there checked the paperwork and soon a truck delivered the merchandise to the Hotel Carleton Elite. What I saw next would have had most people pull their hair out of their head. Some of the goods were badly crushed in the boxes, but I had a trick… I hung the goods up in the bathroom on the water pipe, ran the hot water and the steam soon straightened out the creases. The coats looked brand new. People often asked how it was that everyone else's coats were crushed and mine were fresh. I told them that it was because of the way I packed them! I did not tell my secret.

Next morning I called to make appointments to see some people in Zurich I had not seen yet, and some people from Basel. Everyone seemed to like me and most of all liked what I was selling. Some people bought five or six coats at a time. I had some jackets with me too, but most of the sales were for long coats and three quarter coats.

After that, we returned to Lausanne to make appointments to see more furriers. One was *Benjamin Furs* and the other was *Bosdigan*. I had heard that Mr. Benjamin was very important and rich and very tough to do business with. The De La Paire hotel manager, a very decent person, seeing the number tattooed on my arm allowed me to use a room upstairs as a showroom.

I went downstairs to the lobby to meet Mr. Benjamin. The model pointed him out for me. He was standing with a woman, whom he introduced as his daughter-in-law. They came up to my showroom: Mr. Benjamin, a Sephardic Jew in his late seventies, and the daughter-in-law, a Jewess from Egypt and a tough businesswoman.

The daughter-in-law seemed upset that Mr. Benjamin and I were getting on so well and she left. Mr. Benjamin and I talked and joked and then we got down to business. Every garment had a ticket and if he liked it he put some kind of mark on it with his fingernail. A trick that I knew from old! "OK," he said, "these pieces and two sable coats. Bring them up to my house."

And what a house he had! Set in a beautiful location in Lausanne right on the lake. Not only did it have five floors with an elevator, it also had a separate temple with five *Sefer Torahs*. Later, when I went to Lausanne and was stuck for the Jewish holidays, he would insist that I go to his house for the whole day and *daven* (pray) and eat with them. I was made very welcome there. People did not believe how well we got along, because he had a tough reputation.

When I came to his house, the driver took the coats and threw them on the floor; in the fur business, everyone did that. Benjamin counted the coats and asked how much it came to. When I told him the price, he just smiled. I looked at him and said, "I'm giving you a good price." "Take off 5,000 francs and you've got a deal!" he said. I sighed and then nodded. We took the elevator upstairs to his room. It was a small room with a bed. He said, "sit down". "Where?" I asked. "On the bed. How do you want to get paid, Swiss francs or a check?" "Anything you say is good for me". Benjamin replied, "I will give you Swiss francs, ok?" What could I say, no? I said, "However you want it Mr. Benjamin!"

I stood in his bedroom and watched, as he took a box out from under his bed and started counting Swiss francs, big bills right in front of me more than 180,000 Swiss francs. After he paid me, he walked over to a cabinet and took out two small blue glasses that he said were his grandfather's (my father used to have such glasses too). "Shalom, let's drink *l'chaim*!", (to life) he said. Then he filled the glasses and we made *l'chaim*. If I had been invited to meet the President I could not have felt better than I did at that moment.

The next day I managed to sell some pieces to Bosdigan; he paid me right away, and three or four pieces to the Frenchman. With the goods I had left, I went to Geneva and to a store over there, I knew the owner from New York. She knew the quality of my stuff and bought several pieces. After that I sold some merchandise to a Jewish guy named Levin. I had done very well and decided to go back to Zurich. This was the beginning of my big business in Europe.

Chapter 18
Farewell, My Love

In Munich there was a company by the name of Peltshouse Reiger that made plates from Persian Lamb paws, before the war. Hertz Reiger came from a small town in Galicia, Ravaruska. Before the war, he came to Warsaw as a barefoot youngster looking for a job. Some furriers told him that he would find a good job over at Silberzweigs. "They make a lot of Persians and they get paws. You should be able to do that over there," they said. My mother took pity on this motherless boy, and cooked wonderful things for him, like he was one of her own. She would always give him the best part of the meal.

Years passed, and one day Reiger found out that there was a very successful businessman in New York by the name of Silberzweig. He arranged for some friends of his to get in touch with me. "Sure I know Hertz," I told them. "Get in touch with him, sure I will!" And I thought that would be the end of that.

Switzerland was a small country and I had sold merchandise to almost every furrier. I made a few inquiries of my own and found out that Reiger ran a very big business, one of the largest in Europe. I decided to call him up from Zurich. I told him my name and that I was Yossel Silberzweig's son. "*Oy, Oy. Der kleiner?*" (the youngest?) He said. He wanted to know how things were with me. I just said that I was making very nice mink furs. "Come over here," he said. I told him that I did not want to go to Germany, but he said, "Come, on, everything's OK here. People come from all over the world to see me." He tried to convince me to come by telling me that he would buy everything I had and how I could ship the goods to Munich. He also told me how to take the goods out.

At this point I had about thirty-seven coats left out of the hundred and I was tempted by his offer, but I had always promised myself I would never go back to Germany. Now I decided that I **would** go to Germany, and ship the goods to Munich through my agent at Natural. When I arrived, I met Reiger in his store. I could not believe it, it was like twenty stores rolled into one. It was enormous. He was obviously a very generous employer; he had a bar and restaurant right on the premises for the thirty or forty workers he employed.

Reiger was eager to see the furs I had brought, but first I had to release them. He asked if I had an agent and I told him yes. In Germany you have to leave collateral with customs to release the goods. But there was no need for me to worry, my agent took care of this.

The goods released, I hung them up in his store. "So how many pieces have you got?" he asked. I told him thirty-seven. "OK," he said. "I'll take the lot." He sent his accountant with me to the bank. After we came back, Reiger said, "Right, business over, now we go out for dinner!"

The next day I was invited to Reiger's villa. I thought Mr. Benjamin had a huge house but that was nothing compared with Reiger's home, it was as big as a castle. He had a tennis court, a bowling alley and a swimming pool – both indoors and out. There was also a statue of

Moses with the Ten Commandments. Unbelievable!

After that, I did tremendous business with Reiger –more than a million dollars of business every year, as regular as clockwork. All this business came about as a result of Reiger having been given a chance by my family when he was young.

We continued to do business right up until 1991. All the skin dealers were very jealous. No one knew how we became so close. In 1991, I stopped going to Europe. There was too much competition from Greece. They made the mink garments and brought them to Germany. I felt that the last couple of trips no longer paid, and I stopped going altogether.

I had done well all over Germany – in Frankfurt, Keln, Essen and more. I had sold a lot of merchandise, made a lot of money and met many people who liked me. I also had done very well in Switzerland, Italy and France. I even had customers in Israel. In Frankfurt's fair the great fashion house of none other than Christian Dior ordered about thirty or forty coats from me. At one time I had twenty-five people working for me in the factory making coats. I had a designer in Bologna, Italy "Denati Modella." We worked together, forty-five days at a time developing styles. I had an excellent designer in New York named Johnny Pecarella who took the European designs and developed them into an American fit. It was different than the European. We were very successful. People could not believe how I had such beautiful designs every time.

* * * * * *

The people with whom I did business in Switzerland told me about the *Frankfurter messer*, the fair in Germany. They felt I would be a great success there. I did not need much persuasion, and put together a collection of several hundred, maybe 400 units, every show requiring different furs. It was usual for me to go to fur fairs with Gloria and this time was no different. Reiger and other customers in Munich had picked out some merchandise in the fair and so we headed for Munich to deliver the goods and get paid. I had a policy to deliver the merchandise and get paid on delivery when we finished the Frankfurt business.

I was driving back on the Autobahn, to head straight back to Frankfurt after making the delivery in Munich. We had made this trip after the fair many times before. As usual, Gloria and I fought about her refusal to put on her seat belt; she liked to smoke in the car and did not want to be buckled in. We stopped a few times to have a coffee and fill up with gas. It was midday on May 15, 1979, a beautiful clear day with no traffic. A sign up ahead warned that the road was under repair and that we had to go around. It was a three-lane road and I was in the first lane next to the divider. I was just preparing to go straight ahead around the repair crew when all of a sudden there was a loud bang. A car had hit us from the right hand side. My car started to spin round fast, completely out of control. Somewhere it seemed in the distance I could hear the sound of trucks passing. I looked down at my hand; blood was flowing. Then, the whole world twisting and turning, I went in and out of consciousness.

When truck drivers took me out of the car, they covered me with vests that had oil stains on, to stop the bleeding from my hand. Later it caused gangrene.

An ambulance was taking me to a hospital. "What happened?" I remembered asking over and over again. "What happened?" I looked down at my bloodied hand covered in dirty pieces of cloth. I was feeling *farmished* (confused). "Gloria, where's Gloria?" I kept asking. I was taken to a hospital in Schaffenburg and put into a room with eight people. "My wife, where's Gloria?" I continued to ask. Finally, someone told me that she was in The Ladies Hospital. It was later that I found out the horrific truth.

Unbeknown to me, it was all over the radio how Sol Silberzweig from America was traveling on the autobahn and lost his wife in a car accident. A good friend called my agent in Frankfurt and told him what had happened; immediately he arranged for me to be put in a private room. I had not been in the private room five minutes when some nurses came and took me down to the operating room. The head doctor, the director general of the hospital, already had left and went home. As I was lying on the operating table, I heard two doctors discussing me: "How far are we going to cut his arm?" All of a sudden I heard the telephone ring. Later I was told that the head doctor had called and told the doctors in the hospital not to cut anything and instead to try and heal my wounds. He told them to wait for him to come back. Now I was being treated well. The head doctor came and took me again to the operating room. He decided not to operate, but instead to try to clean the gangrene.

My brother, daughter Shelley and son came to the

hospital to see me. Jack never wanted to come back to Germany, but this news brought him back. I kept asking where Gloria was and they just kept telling me she was in a different hospital. I believed them. I had no reason not to.

A few days later a friend of mine, Yasha Weiner, a skin dealer from Frankfurt, came to visit me. I told him that Gloria was in another hospital. Straight away he said, "Gloria *is nisht du mer*." ("Gloria is gone.") I could not believe it, I was furious. That was how I found out the devastating news that Gloria had been thrown through the windshield and died instantly from her injuries. The man who crashed into me ran away.

I hired the top lawyer in Munich to try to find him. Finally, they found out that the man belonged to the German government in Bonn and they were covering up for him. I hired another lawyer to try to pursue the case, but the lawyer said I should let it go. "You've got the insurance money," he said. I told him that it was not about the money.

Later in the hospital, my hand, broken in three places, started to heal. The doctor said "We will put it in a temporary cast so you will be able to go home."

My wife was gone and I was left with a hole in my heart. A rabbi in New York talked to me and explained, that G-d wanted it to be this way and you cannot fight that. A priest told me the same thing. This did not stop the pain I was feeling. I had known this beautiful woman since she was twelve years old.

I wanted to bring Gloria's body back to the United States after the accident, but it was not that easy, there was a lot of paperwork to complete. My friend Yasha

Weiner had connections with the Governor in Frankfurt, so he took care of the permit that was needed to take a body outside the country. Once I was back in America I had to arrange for her *levaya* (funeral). My brother belonged to a famous *shul* (synagogue) in Teaneck, New Jersey. I bought four plots, for my brother, for me, for Gloria and for my brother's wife. Gloria of course got the first plot.

When we came back from the funeral, we went to my brother's house where people were eating, drinking and talking. I just wanted to go home to start sitting *shiva*. In the meantime, everyone in the fur market was saying that I was crippled, that I would not be able to work and I would not be doing business anymore. I was still a young man and even though I was admitted into Mount Sinai hospital to continue treatment for my arm, I was determined that I was going to get on with my life.

Broken in three places, I had to wear my arm in a sling for months. I was in a lot of pain but I was given painkillers to ease it a little. A doctor operated to fix the broken bones and another doctor worked on the skin. The doctor who operated on my arm worked hard to fix it; he said it was in a terrible state. He had been a Colonel in the army and knew about Dachau and understood what I had been through. He was a wonderful man, an angel. He had an office on 72nd street, and Park Avenue. They sent me for physical therapy at 1100 Park Avenue, to help with my finger, which was paralyzed. Even though I was starting to feel much better, I had to continue having treatment. They grafted skin from my left leg on my arm. I was in terrible pain and it took months to heal.

My arm in a cast, I went back to the market. I said to myself, "Sol, what are you going to do with yourself sitting at home?" It had been several months since the accident, my fingers were working, and my broken heart was just beginning to heal. By 1980 I was strong and powerful again and I decided to go back to the business, which kept going even though I was not there. The people I knew, especially friends of Gloria could not do enough for me. When the people saw me in the market, they were surprised that I was not a cripple in a wheelchair.

I started to prepare a line and have continued up until today, for I am still in the business.

It was in 1983, while I was with my collection in Geneva, that I got a call from America that my brother Jack had passed away in the middle of the night. Two weeks earlier his daughter had died of cancer. He had taken it so much to heart that he died too. I left my business with my model and driver, and that same day flew back to New York.

Friends and family, including his son, who had become a professor of psychology in Canada, packed the same funeral parlor. We took Jack's body to the cemetery and buried him. He was buried next to the plot I bought because his daughter was buried in the plot that was planned for him. Then we sat *shiva*. He was eighty-two years old when he died. This was the last brother I had. Now the whole family was gone.

* * * * * *

On December 21, 1988, I was on my way back from Europe to New York. I was late arriving at the airport and missed my flight. This was Pan Am flight 103 which crashed around Lockerbie, Scotland that evening because of a terrorist's bomb. My luck had not run out yet.

Sol with David Santzer

Sol and Gloria

Seder with the family

*Kielce,
after the war*

Kielce

Sabina & David Reicher
Lynn & Bernard Rosenblum
Albert Scheintaub
Sheila & Abraham Schlussel
Gitel & Shalom Silberzweig
Edita & Abraham Spiegel
Frances & Arthur Urwitz
Benjamin Weiss

Stone at Yad Vashem

Sol and Avner Shalev at Yad Vashem

Epilogue

As I look back on my life, I realize that from my whole family I am the sole survivor. I recall how they disappeared. How they were tricked and gassed. I was in the Warsaw Ghetto. I survived seven concentration camps. They weren't work camps. They were the worst camps that existed. Yet why did I survive and others from my family perished? Was it a miracle? I asked a rabbi friend of mine why I had survived and others had died. He said because that is the way G-d wanted it to be.

I came out of the camps with nothing in my pocket, only my striped uniform. I was able to make a big success of myself and be happy with friends all over the world; everyone thinks I am a genius because of what I managed to achieve.

It's so sad that nobody else from my immediate family was able to make it, to join in my success and be happy for me. After having gone through so much trouble to survive I lost my wife in a terrible car accident; the girl I loved so much. We were as close as if we were glued together, and she was taken from me, and when she died it broke my heart.

I loved her so much I never married again. To think she survived the concentration camps and then was killed in a road accident – and in Germany! She died and I was injured in my mind and body. Two doctors in the hospital were ready to amputate my arm when a call came to tell them not to, but to treat the wound instead. Had the call come in later, they would have cut my hand off. It was a miracle.

My survival was due in part to my ability to think ahead of what I needed to do in order to be able to survive. The second part was luck and a big miracle.

I would like to go over some of the events I was lucky enough to overcome:

When they took everyone away from Schultz to the Kotchl, I thought how I could put together a plan to enable me to bring my family back from there. My plan was successful and I saved them… at least for a while. In the end, all but Gloria perished.

During the Warsaw Ghetto uprising I lived through hell. When I was in Birkenau, there were maybe 10,000 to 15,000 people there. One time they came to ask for people to work; from all the people in the camp they picked thirty-eight people and I was one of the thirty-eight.

Mauthausen was one of the worst camps that existed. People died there like flies because of the terrible freezing cold; it was something like 35°F below zero. People were forced to stand outside in the bitter cold for an hour after work, and every day three to four people died. This was done purposely.

I was lucky, I noticed the block *eldester* was wearing sheepskin gloves and I had the nerve to offer to make him newer and nicer gloves. I gambled on my life when I told him that if he didn't like the gloves he could kill me! This saved my life once again.

I was in the hands of Mengele, and escaped, as a result of another stroke of luck.

It was November and I was in Birkenau working for the *trupen lazare*t putting in sewer lines on the outside. Every morning everyone would go to work; that meant standing in a lot of water. It was winter and it was cold, but I managed to organize a warm coat to wear and nice shoes. You had to organize things for yourself otherwise you didn't get anything.

In the camp at Lagisha where they built electricity plants, I was hungry and cold and I told myself that I wouldn't be able to go on much longer. I didn't want to give up. With my unbelievable *chutzpah*, I bribed the doctor in this camp with a gold watch. Under his instruction, I fooled the SS into thinking I was sick and the doctor sent me back to Auschwitz.

In 1945, I was on a death march. My life was saved by underground people who pretended to be German and turned the death march around, and again by the guard's girlfriend who talked him out of killing us, because she was afraid of retribution.

When I escaped from the death march, the Germans fired at me with their machine guns but missed.

To survive everything I went through: the seven camps, the Warsaw Ghetto, the factories, the uprising, and the death marches was a combination of unbelievable luck and a tremendous will to survive which gave me unusual strength.

On May 1, 1945 when I was liberated by the Americans, I felt I had been reborn, just born that day, and now I had to start life again, a better life. I know that G-d gave me back my life to start over.

When the war ended, I decided to look for my girl-friend, not knowing if she survived, and after a long search, I found Gloria again. When I found my future wife I felt I was born a third time.

I built a successful business in Germany and then I

came to the United States and started to build another business. At first things were hard but then it became easier. I built up a name in the fur business not only in the United States, but also all over the world; I was known as *Royal Mink*.

I traveled to many countries to buy the raw furs and worked with my designer in Italy to make a quality product. I made mostly minks, but also sables and other furs.

When I became comfortable, I decided to donate part of my wealth to organizations that would make sure the six million Jews murdered in the Holocaust would never be forgotten. I was one of the founders of the Holocaust Museum in Washington; I also made a large donation to Yad Vashem. I am donating a statue commemorating Auschwitz that will be placed in the new Historical Museum at Yad Vashem.

It is my feeling that this very important institution will always remind the children and grandchildren, and the whole world what happened. I also decided to support the Warsaw Ghetto Resistance organization.

Finally, I support the Israeli Defense Forces. I feel that every Jew should do the same, because without a strong Israel all Jews all over the world can never feel safe. People should use their money for good will.

I felt that I must write my story, not just for my children and their children to read and understand, but for the whole world to know what happened in those dark, dark days, and I hope and pray that it will never happen again.

Sol Silberzweig, 2004